WOMEN,

THEIR LIVES & LOVES, IN
THE SCRIPTURES
A REFERENCE BOOK WITH
FASCINATING READING

COMPILED BY

CHARLES DOUGLAS GREER

Bloomington, IN Milton Keynes, UK

authorHOUSE®

AuthorHouse™
1663 Liberty Drive, Suite 200
Bloomington, IN 47403
www.authorhouse.com
Phone: 1-800-839-8640

AuthorHouse™ UK Ltd.
500 Avebury Boulevard
Central Milton Keynes, MK9 2BE
www.authorhouse.co.uk
Phone: 08001974150

First published by AuthorHouse 11/30/2006

ISBN: 1-4259-6373-0 (sc)
ISBN: 1-4259-6374-9 (dj)

Library of Congress Control Number: 2006908746

Printed in the United States of America
Bloomington, Indiana

This book is printed on acid-free paper.

WOMEN

THEIR LIVES
&
LOVES,

IN THE SCRIPTURES.

A REFERENCE BOOK WITH FASCINATING READING BIBLE CHAPTERS WITHIN PARENTHESIS, ALPHABETIZED AND CHRONICLED, IN REGARDS TO THE EVENTS OF THE INDIVIDUAL.

FROM THE KING JAMES VERSION OF THE BIBLE.

Also

THE BOOK OF JASHER.

COMPILED BY

CHARLES DOUGLAS GREER

187 WOMEN LISTED

LILITH
(The First Woman)
Hebrew Bible:
3761bc.

She is found in Jewish literature where it is said that she was Adams' first wife.

A contradiction in that the Hebrew Bible has her born 243 years after Eve was born.

God had decided to create a companion for Adam. He created her in the same manner that He created Adam, out of earth.

She and Adam argued right from the start because she would not do Adams' bidding. Because of this she was expelled from the Garden of Eden. She had, however, slept with Adam and gave birth to "evil spirits".

Adam called upon God to bring her back. But she refused.

God sent three angels after her. Still she refused to go back to Adam and vowed she would harm newborn children, male and female alike.

She became a succubus, "a demon who gave birth of witches." An incubus having intercourse with men while they slept.

Some Jewish historians believe she is mentioned in **Isaiah 34:14,** where she is said to be the "screech-owl".

In other writings, she is referred to as a "night hag" and an enemy of newborn children.

She is also found in Babylonian myth.

She was said to of been married to Satan.

Others say she was the wife of Samael, Angel of Death.

ABI

726bc.

(331) 2 KINGS 18:2 Twenty and five years old was he when he began to reign; and he reigned twenty and nine years in Jerusalem. His mother's name also was **Abi** the daughter of Zachariah.

ABIAH

1471bc.

(334) 1 CHRON 2:24. And after that Hezron was dead in Calebephratah, and **Abiah,** Hezron's wife bare him Ashur the father of Tekoa.

ABIGAIL

(Wife of Nabal)

1060bc.

(281) 1 Samuel 25:3 "Now the name of the man was Nabal; and the name of his wife **Abigail**; and she was a woman of good understanding and of a beautiful countenance: but the man (her husband) was churlish and evil in his doings; and he was of the house of Caleb."

1053bc.

(270) 2 Sam. 3:3 "And his second, Chileab, of **Abigail** the wife of Nabal the Carmelite, and the third, Absalon the son of Maacah, the daughter of Talmai king of Geshur;"

ABIGAIL 2

(Wife of Jether)

1023bc.

(284) 2 Samuel 17:25 "And Absalom made Amasa captain of the host instead of Joab: which Amasa was a man's son whose name Ithra, an Israelite, that went in to Abigail the daughter of Nahash, sister to Zeruiah, Joab's mother."

1471bc.

(340) 1 CHRON. 2:16 "Whose sisters were Zeruiah, and **Abigail**. And the sons of Zeriah; Abishai, and Joab, and Asahel, three.

1 CHRON. 2:17 "And Abigail bare Amasa: and the father of Amasa was Jether the Ishmaelite."

(341) 1 CHRON.3:1 "Now these were the sons of David, which were born unto him in Hebron; the first-born Amnon, of Ahinoam the Jereelitess; the second, Daniel, of Abigail the Carmelitess:

ABIHAIL

Abishur's wife.

1471bc.

(340) 1 CHRON. 2:29. And the name of the wife of Abishur was **Abihail**; and she bare him Ahban, and Mobid.

ABIHAIL 2

Rehoboam's wife.

974bc.

(349) 11 CHRON.11:18. And Rehoboam took him Mahalath the daughter of Jerimoth the son of David to wife, and **Abihail** the daughterof Eliab the son of Jesse;

ABIJAH

741bc

(396) 2 CHRON. 29:1. Hezekiah began to reign when he was five and twenty years old, and he reigned nine and twenty years in Jerusalem. And his mother'sname was Abijah the daughter of Zechariah.

ABISHAG

1015bc.

(292) 1 KINGS. 1:3. "So they sought for a fair damsel throughout all the coasts of Israel and found **Abishag** a Shunammite, and they brought her to the king."

1 KINGS. 1:15. "And Bath-sheba went unto the king into the chamber; and the king was very old; and **Abishag** the Shunammite ministered unto the king."

1014bc.

(293) 1 KINGS. 2:17 "And he said, speak, I pray thee, unto Solomon the king (for he will not say nay,) that he give **Abishag** the Shunammite to wife."

1 KINGS. 2:21. "And she said, Let **Abishag** the Shunammite be given to Adononijah thy brother to wife."

1 KINGS. 2:22. "And king Solomon answered and said unto his mother, And why dost thow ask **Abishag** the Shunammite for Adonijah? Ask him the kingdom also;"

ABITAL

1058bc.

(270) 2 SAM. 3:4. "And the fourth, Adonijah the son of Haggith; and the fifth, Shephatiah the son of **Abital**;"

1471bc.

(341) 1 CHRON. 3:3. "The fifth, Shephatiah of **Abital**: the sixth, Ithream by Eglah his wife."

ACHSAH

1444bc.

(202) JOSH. 15:16. "And Caleb said, He that smiteth Kirjathsepher, and taketh it, to him will I give **Achsah** his daughter to wife."

JOSH. 15:17. "And Othniel the son of Kenaz, the brother of Caleb, took it; and he gave **Achsah** his daughter to wife."

1425bc.

(212)JUDG. 1:12. "And Caleb said, He that samiteth Kirjathsepher, and taketh it, to him I will give **Achsah** my daughter to wife."

JUDG. 1:13. "And Othniel the son of Kenaz, Caleb's yunger brother, took it, and he gave **Achsah** his daughter to wife."

1471bc.

(340) 1 CHON. 2:49. "She bare also Shaaph the father of Madmannah, Sheva the father Machbenah, and the fatherof Gibea: and the daughter of Caleb was **Achsah**."

ADAH

The wife of Lamech.

3875bc.

(4) Gen.4:19 "And Lamech took unto him two wives: the name of theone was **Adah** and the name of the other Zilla."

Gen.4:20 "And Adah bare Jabal: he was the father of such as dwell in tents, and of sush as have cattle."

Gen,4:23 "And Lamech said unto his wives, **Adah** and Zillah, Here my voice, ye wives of Lemech, hearken unto my speech: for I have slain a man to my wounding, and a young man to my hurt."

ADAH 2

Esau's wife.

1796bc.

(36) Gen, 36:2 "Esau took his wives of the daugthters of Canaan; **Adah** the daughter of Elon the Hittite , and Aholibamah the daughter of Anah the daughter of Zibeon the Hivite."

Gen.36:4 "And **Adah** bare to Esau, Eliphaz; and Bathemath, bare Reuel;

GEN.36:16 "Duke Korah, duke   Gatam, and duke Amalek: these are the dukesthat came of Eliphaz, in the land of Edom: these were the sons of **Adah**.

AHINOAM

The Jezeelitess.

1471BC.

(341) 1 CHRON. 3:1. "Now these were the sons of David, which were born unto him in Heron; the first-born Amnon, of Ahinoam the Jezeelitess; the second, Daniel, of Abigail the Carmelitess;"

AHINOAM 2

Saul's wife

1087bc.

(250) 1 SAM. 14:50. "And the name Saul's wife was Ahinoam, the daughter of Ahimaaz: and the nane of the captain of his host was Abner, son of Ner, Saul,s uncle."

AHINOAM 3
David's wife

1060bc.

(261) 1 SAM. 25:43. "David also took **Ahinoam** of Jezreel; and they were also both of them his wives."

1058bc.

(263) 1 SAM. 27:3. "And David dwelt with Achish at Gath, he and his men, every man with his household, even David with his two wives, **Ahinoam** the Jezreelitess, and Abigail the Carmelitess, Nabal's wife."

1056bc.

(266) 1 SAM. 30:5. "And David's two wives were taken captives, **Ahinoam** the Jezreelitess, and Abigail the wife of Nabal the Carmeketite."

(269) 2 SAM. 2:2. "So David went up thither, and his two wives also, **Ahinoam** the Jezeelitess and ABIGAIL Nabal's wife the Camelite."

AHLAI

1471bc.

(340) 1 CHRON. 2:31 "And the sons of Appaim; Ishi. And the sons of Ishi ; Sheshan. And the "children of Sheshan; **Ahlai**".

AHOLAH

598bc.

(825) **EZEK. 23:4.** "And the names of them were **Aholah** the elder, and Aholibah her sister; and they were mine, and they bare sons and daughters. Thus were their names; **Aholah**, and Aholibah."

EZEK. 23:5. "**Aholah** played the harlot when she was mine; and she doted on her lovers, on the Assyrian her neighbours."

EZEK. 23:7. "Thus she committed her whoredoms with them, with all of them that were the chosen menof Assyria, and with all that on whom she doted; with all their idols she defiled herself."

EZEK. 23:36. "The Lord said, moreover, unto me; Son of man, wilt thou judge **Aholah** and AHOLIBAH? Yea, declare unto them their abominations;

EZEK. 23:44. "Yet they went in unto her, as they go in unto a woman that played the harlot: so went they in unto **Aholah** and unto Aholibah, the lewd women.

AHOLIBAH

(825) EZEK. 23:4. "And the names of them were Aholah the elder, and **Aholibah** her sister; and they were mine, and they bare sons and daughters. This were their names; Aholah, and **Aholibah.**"

EZEK. 23:11. "And when her sister **Aholibah** saw this, she was more corrupt in her inordinate love than she, and in her whoredoms more than her sister in her whoredoms."

EZEK. 23:22. "Therefore, O **Aholibah**, thus saith the Lord God; Behold, I well raise up thy lovers against thee, from whom thy mind is alienated, and I will bring them against thee on every side;"

EZEK. 23:36. "The Lord said, moreover, unto me; Son of man, wilt thou judge Aholah and **Aholibah** ? yea,declare unto them their abominations;"

EZEK. 23:44. "Yet they went in unto her, as they go in unto a woman that played the harlot: so went they in unto Aholah and unto **Aholibah**, the lewd women."

AHOLIBAMAH

1796bc.

(36) GEN. 36:2. "Esau took his wives of the daughters of Canaan; Adah the daughter of Elon the Hittite, and **Aholibamah** the daughter of ANAH the daughter of Zibeon Hivite;"

1760bc.

GEN. 36:5. "And **Aholibamah** bare Jeush, which were born unto him in the land of Canaan."

GEN. 36:14. "And these were the sons of **Aholibamah**, the daughter of Anah, the daughter of Zibeon, Esau's wife: and she bare to Esau, Jeush, and Jaalam, and Korah."

1715bc.

GEN. 36:18. "And these are the sons of **Aholibamah**, Esau's wife; duke Jeush, duke Jaalam, duke Korah: these were the dukes that came of **Aholibamah** the daughter of Anah, Esau's wife."

1840bc.

GEN. 36:25. "And the children of Anah were these; Dishon, and Aholibamah the daughter of Anah. "

ANAH

1775bc.

(36) GEN. 36:2. "Esau took his wives of the daughters of Canaan; Adah the daughter of Elon the Hittite, and Aholibamah the daughter of **ANAH** The Daughter of Zibeon Hivite;"

1715bc.

GEN. 36:14. "And these were the sons of Aholibamah, the daughter of Anah, the daughter of Zibeon, Esau's wife: and she bare to Esau, Jeush, and Jaalam, and Korah."

1725bc.

GEN. 36:18. "And these are the sons of Aholibamah, Esau's wife; duke Jeush, duke Jaalam, duke Korah: these were the dukes that came of Aholibamah the daughter of **Anah**, Esau's wife."

1760bc.

GEN. 36:24. "And these are the children of Zibeon; both Ajah, and **Anah**: this was that **Anah** that found the mules in the wilderness, as he fed the asses of Zibeon his father."

ANNA

**Before the Account
called Anno Domimi
the fourth year.**

(975) LUKE. 2:36 "And there was one **Anna**, a prophetess, the daughter of Phanuel, of the tribe of Aser: she was of great age, and had lived with an husband seven years from her virginity;"

12

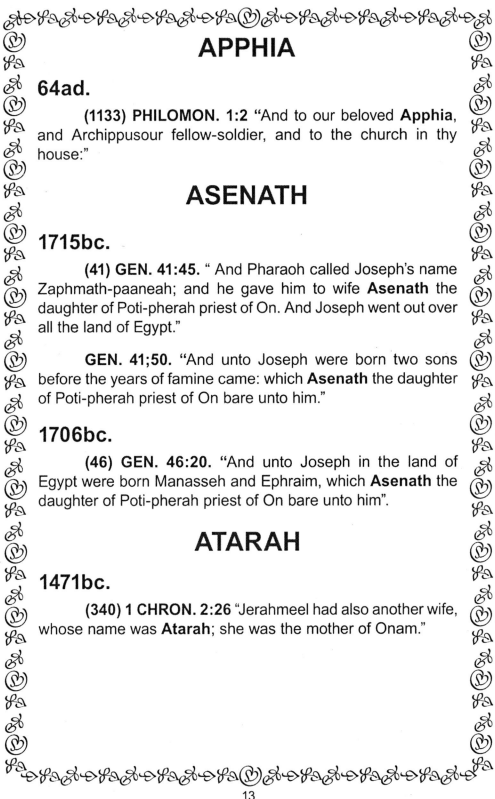

APPHIA

64ad.

(1133) PHILOMON. 1:2 "And to our beloved **Apphia**, and Archippusour fellow-soldier, and to the church in thy house:"

ASENATH

1715bc.

(41) GEN. 41:45. " And Pharaoh called Joseph's name Zaphmath-paaneah; and he gave him to wife **Asenath** the daughter of Poti-pherah priest of On. And Joseph went out over all the land of Egypt."

GEN. 41;50. "And unto Joseph were born two sons before the years of famine came: which **Asenath** the daughter of Poti-pherah priest of On bare unto him."

1706bc.

(46) GEN. 46:20. "And unto Joseph in the land of Egypt were born Manasseh and Ephraim, which **Asenath** the daughter of Poti-pherah priest of On bare unto him".

ATARAH

1471bc.

(340) 1 CHRON. 2:26 "Jerahmeel had also another wife, whose name was **Atarah**; she was the mother of Onam."

ATHALIAH

885bc.

(331) **2 KINGS. 8:26.** Two and twenty years old was Ahaziah when he began to reign and he reigned one year in Jerusalem. And his mother's name was **Athaliah**, the daughter of Omri king of Israel.

885bc.

(389) 2 CHRON. 22:2. "Fourty and two years old was Ahaziah when he began to reign and he reigned one year in Jerusalem. His mother's name also was **Athaliah** the daughter of Omri."

884bc

(324) 2 KINGS. 11:3. "And he was with her in the house of the Lord six years. And **Athaliah** did reign over the land."

(389) 2 CHRON. 22:10. "But when **Athaliah** the mother of Ahaziah saw that her son was dead , she arose, and destroyed all the seed royal of the house of Judah."

2 CHRON. 22:11 "But Jehoshabeath, the daughter of the king took Joash the son of Ahaziah, and stole him from among the king's sons that were slain, and put him and his nurse in a bed- chamber. So Jehoashabeath, the daughter of king Jehoram, the wife of Jehoiada the priest, (for she was the sister of Ahaziah,) hid him from **Athaliah**, so that she slew him not."

2 CHRON. 22:12. "And he was with them hid in the house of God six years: and **Athaliah** reigned over the land."

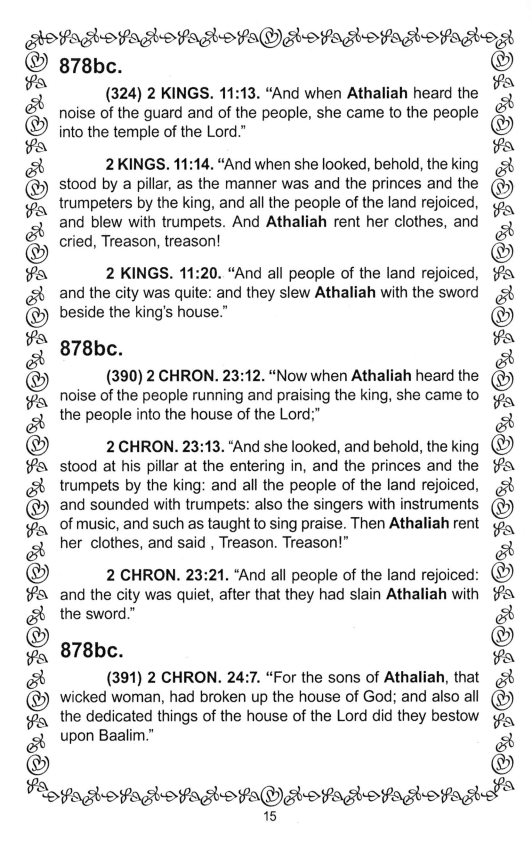

878bc.

(324) 2 KINGS. 11:13. "And when **Athaliah** heard the noise of the guard and of the people, she came to the people into the temple of the Lord."

2 KINGS. 11:14. "And when she looked, behold, the king stood by a pillar, as the manner was and the princes and the trumpeters by the king, and all the people of the land rejoiced, and blew with trumpets. And **Athaliah** rent her clothes, and cried, Treason, treason!

2 KINGS. 11:20. "And all people of the land rejoiced, and the city was quite: and they slew **Athaliah** with the sword beside the king's house."

878bc.

(390) 2 CHRON. 23:12. "Now when **Athaliah** heard the noise of the people running and praising the king, she came to the people into the house of the Lord;"

2 CHRON. 23:13. "And she looked, and behold, the king stood at his pillar at the entering in, and the princes and the trumpets by the king: and all the people of the land rejoiced, and sounded with trumpets: also the singers with instruments of music, and such as taught to sing praise. Then **Athaliah** rent her clothes, and said , Treason. Treason!"

2 CHRON. 23:21. "And all people of the land rejoiced: and the city was quiet, after that they had slain **Athaliah** with the sword."

878bc.

(391) 2 CHRON. 24:7. "For the sons of **Athaliah**, that wicked woman, had broken up the house of God; and also all the dedicated things of the house of the Lord did they bestow upon Baalim."

AZUBAH

Caleb's wife.

1471bc.

(340) 1 CHRON. 2:18. "And Caleb the son of Hezon begat children of **Azubah** his wife, and Jerioth: her son's are Jesher, and Shobab, and Ardon."

1 CHRON. 2:19. "And when **Azubah** was dead, Caleb took unto him Ephrath, which bare him Hur."

AZUBAH 2

Daughter of Shilhi.

914bc.

(313) 1 KINGS. 22:42. "Jehosahaphat was thirty and five years old when he began to reign; and he reigned twenty and five years in Jerusalem. And his mother's name was **Azubah** the daughter of Shilhi."

896bc.

(387) 2 CHRON. 20:31. "And Jehoshaphat reinged over Judah: he was thirty and five years old when he began to reign, and he reigned twenty and five years in Jerusalem. And his mother's name was **Azubah** the daughter of Shilhi."

BAARA

1400bc.

(348) 1 CHRON. 8:8. "And Shaharaim begat children in the country Moab, after he sent them away; Hushim and **Baara** were his wives."

BASHEMATH

1796bc.

(26) GEN.26:34. "And Esau was forty years old when he took to wife Judith the daughter of Beeri the Hittite, and **Bashemath** the daughter of Elon the Hittite."

1760bc.

(36) GEN. 36:4. "And Adah bare Esau, Eliphaz; and **Bashemath** bare Reuel;"

1740bc.

(36) GEN. 36:10. " These are the names of Esau's sons; Eliphaz the son of Adah the wife of Esau; Reuel the son of **Bashemath,** the wife of Esau."

GEN. 36:13. "And these are the sons of Reuel; Nahath, and Zerah, Shammah, and Mizzah: these were the sons of **Bashemath**, Esau's wife. "

1715bc.

GEN. 36:17. " And these are the sons of Reuel, Esau's son; duke Nahath, duke Zerah, duke Shammah, duke Mizzah; these are the duke's that came of Reuel, in the land of Edom: these are the sons of **Bashemath**, Esau's wife."

BASMATH

1014 bc.

(295)1 KINGS 4:15 "Ahimaaz was in Naphtali; he also took **Basmath** the daughter of Solomon to wife".

BATH-SHEBA

1035bc.

(278) 2 Sam. 11:2 "And it came to pass in an evening-tide, that David arose from off his bed, and walked upon the roof of the king's house: and from the roof he saw a woman washing herself; and the woman was very beautiful to look upon"

While bathing in a courtyard pool where she lived in Jerusalem, near the palace, she was spied upon by King David. (Her husband, Uriah was away at the time.) (Later, David had Uriah killed in battle.)

2 Sam. 11:3 (Smitten by her beauty,) " And David sent and inquired after the woman. And one said Is not this **Bath-sheba** the daughter of Eliam, the wife of Uriah the Hittite?

2 Sam. 11:4 "And David sent messengers and took her: and she came in unto him and he lay with her; (for she was purified from her uncleanness:) and she returned unto her house".

2 Sam.11:5 "The woman conceived, and sent and told David, I am with child. The child was Solomon."

1034bc.

2 SAM.12:24. "And David comforted **Bath-Sheba** his wife, and went in unto her, and lay with her: and she bare a son, and he called his name Solomon: and the Lord loved him."

1015bc.

(292) 1 KINGS.1:11. "Wherefore Nathan spake unto **Bath-Sheba** the mother of Solomon, saying, Hast thou not heard that Adonijah, the son of Haggith doth reign, and David our lord knoweth it not ?"

1 KINGS.1:15. "And **Bath-Sheba** went in unto the king into the chamber; and the king was very old; and Abishag the Shunammite ministered unto the king."

1 KINGS.1:16. "And **Bath-Sheba** bowed, and did obeisance unto the king, And the king said, What wouldest thou?"

1 KINGS.1:28. "Then king David answered and said, Call me **Bath-Sheba**. And she came into the king's presence, and stood before the king."

1 KINGS.1:31. "Then Bath-Sheba bowed with her face to the earth, and did reverence to the king, and said, Let my lord king live for ever."

1 KINGS. 2:13. "And Adonijah the son of Haggith came to **Bath-Sheba** the mother of Solomon: and she said, Comest thou, peaceably ? And he said, Peaceably."

1 KINGS. 2:18. "And **Bath-Sheba** said; I will speak for thee unto the king."

1 KINGS. 2:19. "**Bath-Sheba** therefore went unto king Solomon, to speak unto him for Adonijab. And the king rose up to meet her, and bowed himself unto her, and sat down on his throne, and caused a seat to be set for the king's mother; and she sat on his right hand."

BATH-SHUA

1471bc.

(341) **1 CHRON. 3:5.** "And these were born unto him in Jerusalem; Shimea, and Nathan and Solomon, four, of **Bath-SHUA** the daughter of Ammiel:"

BERNICE

62ad.

(1043) ACTS. 25:23. "And on the morrow, when Agrippa was come, and **Bernice**, with great pomp, and was entered into the place of hearing, with the chief captains and principal men of the city, at Festus' commandment Paul was brought forth.

(1044) ACTS. 26:30 "And when he had thus spoken, the king rose up, and the governor, and **Bernice,** and they that sat with them:

BILHAH

1760bc.

(29) GEN. 29:29. "And Laban gave to Rachel his daughter, **Bilhah** his handmaid, to be her maid."

1749bc.

(30) GEN. 30:3. "And she said, Behold my maid **Bilhah**, go in unto her; and she shall bare upon my knees, that I may also have children by her".

GEN. 30:4."And she gave him **Bilhah** her handmade to wife: And Jacob went in unto her."

1748bc.

GEN. 30:5. "And **Bilhah** conceived, and bare Jacob a son."

1747bc.

GEN. 30:7. "And **Bilhah**, Rachel's maid, conceived again, and bair Jacob a second son."

1729bc.

(35) GEN. 35:22. "And it came to pass, when Israel dwelt in that land, that Reuben went and lay with **Bilhah** his father's concubine: And Israel heard it . Now the sons of Jacob were twelve:"

GEN. 35:25. "And the sons of **Bilhah**, Rachel's handmaid; Dan and Naphatli:"

1729bc

(37) GEN. 37:2. "These are the generations of Jacob: Joseph being seventeen years old, was feeging the flock with his brethren; and the lad was with the sons of **Bilhah**, and with the sons Zelpah, his father's wives: and Joseph brought unto his father their evil report."

1706bc.

(46) GEN. 46:25. "These are the sons of **Bilhah,** which Laban gave unto Rachel his daughter, and she bare these unto Jacob: All the souls were seven."

BITHIAH

1300bc.

(342) 1 CHRON. 4:18. "And his wife Jehudijah bare Jered the father of Gedor, and Heber the father of Socho, and Jekuthiel the father of Zanoab. And these are the sons of **Bithiah** the daughter of Pharaoh, which Mered took."

BLACK WOMAN

The only black woman of note that is found in the Bible.

1014bc

(672) SOLOMON'S SONG. 1:5 "I am **black**, but comely, O ye daughters of Jerusalem, as the tents of Kedar, as the curtains of Solomon."

SONG OF SOLOMON. 1:6 "Look not upon me, because I am **black**: my mother's children were angry with me; they made me the keeper of the vineyards; but mine own vinwyards have I not kept."

CAIN'S WIFE

3875bc.

(4) GEN. 4:17. "And **Cain** knew his wife, and she conceived, and bare Enoch: and he builded a city, and called the name of the city after the name of his son, Enoch."

CANDACE

34ad.

(1026) ACTS. 8:27. "And he arose, and went: and behold, a man of Ethiopia, an eunuch of great authority under **Candace** queen of the Ethiopians, who had the charge of all her treasure, and had come to Jerusalem for to worship."

CHLOE

59ad.

(1063) 1 COR. 1:11. "For it hath been declared unto me of you, my brethren, by them which are of the house of **Chloe**, that there are contentions amoung you."

CLAUDIA

66ad.

(1129) 2 TIM. 4:21."Do thy diligence to come before winter. Eubulus greeteth thee, and Pudens, and Linus, and **Claudia**, and all the brethren."

COZBI

1452bc.

(142) **NUM. 25:15,** "And the name of the Midianitish woman that was slain was **Cozbi,** The daughter of Zur; he was hear over a people, and of a chief house in Midian."

NUM. 25:18. "For they vex you with their wiles, where with they have beguiled you in the mater of Peor, and in the mater of **Cozbi**, the daughter of a prince of Midian, their sister, which was alain in the day of the pladue for Peor's sake."

DAMARIS

54ad.

(1035) **ACTS.17:34**. Howbeit, certain men clave unto him, and believed: among the which was Dionysius the Areopagite, and a woman named Damaris, and others with them."

DEBORAH

1336bc.

(215) **Judges, 4:4** "And **Deborah**, a prophetess, wife of Lapidoth, she judged Israel at that time".

(The only woman to hold the position of judge in Israel.)

This was a time when the Canaanites ruled over the Israelites. They were led by General Sisera. For twenty years **Deborah** had a confrountation with the leaders of the Israelites hoping she could extricate them from thier predicament. She called upon Barak, the commander of the army of the Israelites, to assemble ten thousand men.

1296bc.

Jodges, 4:10 "And Barak called Zebulun and Naphtali to Kedesh; and he went up with ten thousand men at his feet : and **Deborah** went up with him"

(216) **Judges, 5:12** "Awake, awake, **Deborah**; awake, awake, utter a song: arise, Barak, and lead thy captivity captive, thou son of Abinoam"

DELILAH

The valley Sorek, where **Delilah** lived, was ruled over by the Philistines whom she was most friendly. Her lover, Samson, was a hero among the Israelites who, at the time, were at war with the Philistines. Many stories were told about his great strength. One of which told of him slaying thousands of Philistines, using only the jawbone of an ass. As **Delilah** was friendly with the Philistines, they're leader sought her help.

1140bc.

(227) JUDGES. 16:4 "And it came to pass afterward, that he loved a woman in the valley of Sorek, whose name was **Dililah**".

Judges, 16:5 "And the lords of the Philistines came unto her, and said unto her, Entice him, and see wherein his great strength lieth, and by what means we may prevail against him, that we may bind him to afflict him: and we will give thee every one of us eleven hundred pieces of silver".

She tried various methods but to no avail. Finely, she used Samson's passion for her.

1120bc

Judges, 16:15 "And she said unto him, How canst thou say, I love thee, when thine heart is not with me? Thou hast mocked me these three times, and hast not told me wherein thy great strength lieth".

Judges, 16:16 "And it came to pass when she pressed him daily with her words, and urged him, so that his soul was vexed unto death"

He then revealed to her that not once had his hair been cut since birth. Should it be cut, he would lose his strength. Soothing Samson to sleep, she then had a servant, quiety, cut off his hair. She had told the Philistines to hide and seize him when his strength had demenished. The philistines did so and **Delilah** claimed her reward."

Judges **16:19** "And she made him sleep upon her knees and she called for a man, and she caused him to shave off the seven locks of his head; and she began to afflict him and his strength went from him.

DINAH

1747bc.

(30) **GEN. 30:21.** "And afterwards she bare a daughter, and called her name **Dinah**"

1732bc.

(34) **GEN. 34:1.** "And **Dinah**, the daugher of Leah, which she bare unto Jacob, went out to see the daughters of the land."

GEN. 34:2. "And when Shechem the son of Hamor the Hivite, prince of the country, saw her, he took her, and lay with her, and defiled her".

Gen. 34:3. "And his soul clave unto Dinah the daughter of Jacob, and he loved the damsel, and spake kindly unto the damsel."

GEN. 34:4 "And Shechem spake unto his father Hamor, saying, Get me this damsel to wife."

GEN. 34:5 And Jacob heard that he had defiled **Dinah** his daughter: (now his sons were with his cattle in the field: and Jacob held his peace until they were come.)"

GEN. 34:13. "And the sons Jacob answered Shechem and Hamor his father deceitfully, and said, because he had defiled **Dinah** their sister:"

Gen. 34:25. "And it came to pass on the third day, when they were sore, that the two sons of Jacob, Simeon and Levi, **Dinah's** brethren, took each man his sword, and came upon the city boldly, and slew all the males."

GEN. 34:26. "And they slew Hamor and Shechem his son with the edge of the sword, and took **Dinah** out of Shechem's house, and went out."

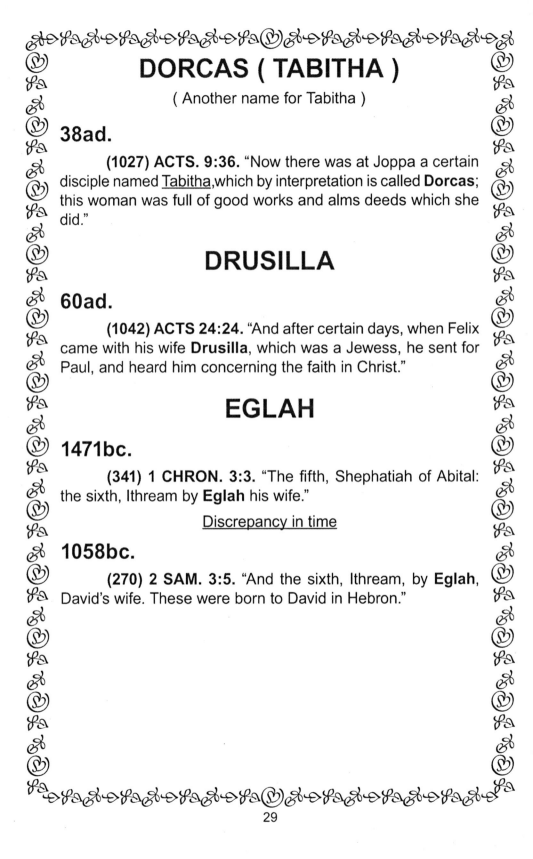

DORCAS (TABITHA)

(Another name for Tabitha)

38ad.

(1027) ACTS. 9:36. "Now there was at Joppa a certain disciple named Tabitha,which by interpretation is called **Dorcas**; this woman was full of good works and alms deeds which she did."

DRUSILLA

60ad.

(1042) ACTS 24:24. "And after certain days, when Felix came with his wife **Drusilla**, which was a Jewess, he sent for Paul, and heard him concerning the faith in Christ."

EGLAH

1471bc.

(341) 1 CHRON. 3:3. "The fifth, Shephatiah of Abital: the sixth, Ithream by **Eglah** his wife."

<u>Discrepancy in time</u>

1058bc.

(270) 2 SAM. 3:5. "And the sixth, Ithream, by **Eglah**, David's wife. These were born to David in Hebron."

ELISABETH

**Before the common
Account called
Anno Domini**

(974) LUKE 1:5. "There was in the days of Herod the king of Judea, a certain priest named Zacharias, of the course of Abia: and his wife was of the daughters of Aaron, and her name was **Elisabeth**."

LUKE 1:13 "But the angel said unto him, Fear not, Zacharias: for thy prayer is heard;and thy wife **Elisabeth** shall bear thee a son, and thou shalt call his name John."

Elisabeth was the wife of a priest called Zacharias. One day while performing his duties in the temple, he was greeted by the angel Gabriel who told him that **Elisabeth** must give birth to a son and that the son must be named John.

Luke 1:20 "And behold thou shalt be dumb, and not able to speak, until the day that these things shall be performed, because thou believest not my word which shall be fulfilled in their season".

He would remain this way until his wife gave birth. He hurried home to tell his wife. But he was without voice so it took him some time to convince Elisabeth that he was not impotent, that he could cause her to conceive. She did conceive and while spending the next few months at home, her cousin, Mary, came to visit her. Mary, at the time, was pregnant with Jesus, but she stayed with Elisabeth throughout her pregnancy.

LUKe 1:24. "And after those days his wife Elisabeth conceived, and hid herself five months, saying,

Luke 1:25 "Thus hath the Lord delt with me in the days wherein he looked on me, to take away my reproach among men."

LUKE 1:36. "And behold, thy cousin **Elisabeth**, she hath also conceived a son in her old age; and this is the sixth month with her who was called barren."

LUKE 1:40. "And entered into the house of Zacharias, and saluted **Elisabeth**."

LUkE, 1:41 "And it came to pass, that when **Elisabeth** heard the salutation of Mary, the babe leaped in her womb: and **Elisabeth** was filled with the Holy Ghost."

After her baby boy was born, she insisted that he be called John. After Zacharias wrote the name on a tablet, he was able to speak again. The child turned out to be John the Baptist.

ELISHEBA

1491bc.

(56) EXOD. 6:23. "And Aaron took him **Elisheba** daughter of Amminadab, sister of Naashon to wife; and she bare him Nadab and Abihu, Eleazar and Ithamar."

EPHAH

1471bc.

(340) 1 CHRON. 2:46. "And **Ephah**, Caleb's concubine, bare Haran, and Moza, and Gazez: and Haran begat Gazez."

EPHRATH

(340) 1 CHRON. 2:19. "And when Azubah was dead, Caleb took unto him **Ephrath,** which bar him Hur."

ESTHER

518bc.

(428) ESTHER 2:7 "And he brought up Hadassah, (that is **Esther,)** his uncle's daughter: for she had neither father nor mother, and the maid was fair and beautiful; whom Mordecai, when her father and mother were dead' took for his own daughter."

510bc.

(433) Esther 7:3. "Then **Esther** the queen answered and said, If I have found favour in thy sight, O king, and if it please the king, let my life be given me at any petition, and my people at my request."

One of the last books to be accepted in the Old Testament. It was accepted by both Jews and Christians. It tells a story of a poor Jewish orphan named **Esther** who lived with her older cousin, Mordecai. When the King of Persia, Ahasurus, (Xerxes 1) was looking for a new queen, **Esther** was chosen from among all the most beautiful maidens of the Persian Empire. She was to replace Queen Vashti once Ahasuerus banished the Queen from his kingdom. The king's chief minister, Haman, finding out that Mordecai was Jewish, plots to distroy him and all of his people. Mordecai talks **Esther** into telling the king what Haman was up too.

Esther 7:10 "So they hanged Haman on the gallows that he had prepared for Mordecai. Then was the king's wrath pacified," Where upon Ahasuerus appoints Mordecai his chief minister. The Jews then carry out a bloody vengeance agenest their enemies throughout the kingdom. Queen **Esther** and Mordecai decree to hold an annual feast of Purim. (Jewish festival. Celebrating the Persian Jews from destruction during the reign of King Ahasuerus.)

EUNICE

66ad.

(1126) **2 TIM. 1:5** "When I call to remembrance the unfeigned faith that is in thee, which dwelt in thy grandmother Lois and thy mother **Eunice**; and I am persuaded that in thee also."

EUODIAS

64ad.

(1107) **PHIL. 4:2** "I beseech **Euodias** and beseech Syntyche ,that they be of the same mind in the Lord."

EVE

4004bc.

Note: The date of 4004 was found written in the margin of a Bible belonging to the archbishop of Amagh, Ireland, in the year of 1650. His name was James Ussher (1581-1656). He had calculated the earth's creation to be 4004 bc.

Another cleric came up with the same date and added the time of day.

9 Am, Oct. the 23rd.

(2) GEN.2:22 "And the rib, which the Lord God had taken from man, made he a woman, and brought her unto the man." In the Christian bible, Genesis says that **Eve** was the first woman whom God created from a rib He had taken from Adam. They both lived in the Garden of Eden where they had all the food they wanted with one exception.

(3) Gen. 3:3 "But of the fruit of the tree which is in the midst of the garden, God hath said, Ye shall not eat of it, neither shall ye touch it, least ye die."

One day **Eve** was sitting under the tree when she heard the hissing of a snake.

Gen.3:4 "And the serpent said unto the woman, Ye shall not surely die." The serpent tried to coax her into eating fruit from the tree.

GEN. 3:6 "And when the woman saw that the tree was good for food; and that it was pleasant to the eyes, and a tree to be desired to make one wise; she took of the fruit there of and did eat; and gave also unto her husband with her, and he did eat".

(4) GEN. 4:1 "And Adam knew Eve his wife, and she conceived, and bare Cain, and said, I have gotten a man from the Lord."

GEN. 4:2 "And she again bare his brother Abel: and Abel was a keeper of sheep, but Cain was a tiller of the ground".

GOMER

785bc.

(863) HOS. 1:3 "So he went and took **Gomer** the daughter of Diblaim; which conceived, and bare him a son."

HADASSAH

518bc.

(428) ESTHER 2:7 "And he brought up **Hadassah**, (that is Ester,) his uncle's daughter: for she had neither father nor mother, and the maid was fair and beautiful;...."

HAGAR

1897bc.

(21) Gen. 21:9 "And Sarah saw the son of **Hagar** the Egyptian, which she had born unto Abraham, mocking."

Gen. 21:14 "And Abraham rose up early in the morning,and took bread, and a bottle of water, and gave it unto **Hagar**, putting it on her shoulder….."

Gen. 21:17 "And God heard the voice of the lad; and the angel of God called to **Hagar** out of heaven, and said unto her, What aileth thee, **Hagar**? Fear not for God has heard the voice of the lad where he is".

Hagar, an Egyptian slave girl, was the handmaiden of Sarah, Abraham's wife. Sarah, unable to have a child, offered **Haga**r to her husband in order for him to have an heir.

Sarah, regretting her decision to lend **Hagar** to Abraharm, became very jealous and abusive toward **Hagar**, who fearing for her life, fled into the desert. There, an angel assured her she would be safe to return. She did so, to give birth to a son, Ishmael.

HAGGITH

1053bc.

(270) 2 SAM. 3:4. "And the fourth, Adomijah the son of Haggith; and the fifth, Shephatiah the son of Abital;"

(341) 1 CHRON. 3:2. "1 CHRON. 3:2. "The third, Absalon the son of Maachah the daughter of Tahmai king of Geshur: the fourth, Adonijah the son of Haggith:"

1015bc.

(292) 1 KINGS.1:5. "Then Adonijh the son of Haggith exalted himself, saying I will be king; and he prepared him chariots and horsemen, and men to run before him."

1 KINGS. 1:11. "Wherefore Nathan spake unto Bath-sheba the mother of Solomon, saying, Hast thou not heard that Adonijah the son of Haggith doth reign, and David our lord knoweth it not?"

(293) 1 KINGS. 2:13. "And Adonijah the son of Haggith came to Bath-Sheba the mother of Solomon: and she said, Comest thou, peaceably ? And he said, Peaceably."

HAMMOLEKETH

1444bc.

(345) 1 CHRON. 7:18. "And his sister Hammoleketh bare Ishod. And Abiezer, and Mahalah.

HAMUTAL

610bc.

(336) 2 KINGS. 23:31. "Jehoahaz was twenty and three years old when he began to reign; and he reigned three months in Jerusalem And his mother's name was **Hamutal**, the daughter of Jeremiah of Libnah."

599bc.

(337) 2 KINGS. 24:18. "Zedekiah was twenty and one years old when he began to reign, and he reigned eleven years in Jerusalem. And his mother's name was **Hamutal**, daughter of Jeremiah of Libnah."

(797) JEREMIAH. 52:1 "Zedekiah was one and twenty years old when he began to reign, and he reigned eleven years in Jerusalem. And his mother's name was **Hamutal** the daughter of Jeremiah of Libnah."

HANNAH

1171bc.

(237) 1 SAM. 1:2. "And he had two wives; the name of the one was **Hannah,** and the name of the other was Peninnah: and Peninnah had children, but **Hannah** had no children."

(237) 1 SAM. 1:5 ."But unto **Hannah** he gave a worthy portion; for he loved **Hannah**; but the lord had shut up her womb.

1 SAM. 1:8. "The said Elkanah her husband to her, **Hannah**, why weepest thou? And why eatest thou not? and why is thy heart grieved? am not I better to thee than ten sons?"

1 SAM. 1:9. "So **Hannah** rose after they had eaten in Shilo, and after they had drunk: (now Eli the priest sat upon a seat by a post of the temple of the Loard:)

1 SAM. 1:13. "Now **Hannah** spake in her heart; only her lips moved, but her voice was not heard: therefore Eli thought she had been drunken."

1 SAM. 1:15. "And **Hannah** answered and said, No, my lord, I am a woman of a sorrowful spirit: I have drunk nether wine nor strong drink, but have poured out my soul before the Lord.

1 SAM. 1:19. "And they rose up in the morrning early, and worshipped before the Lord, and returned, and came to their house to Ramah: and Elkanah knew **Hannah** his wife; and the Lord remembered her."

1 SAM. 1:20. "Wherefore it came to pass, when the time was come about after **Hanna** had conceived, that she bare a son, and called his name Samuel, saying, Because I have asked him of the Lord."

1 SAM. 1:22. "But **Hannah** went not up; for she said unto her husband, I will not go up until the child be weaned, and then I will bring him, that he may appear before the Lord, and there abide for ever."

1 SAM. 2:1. "And **Hannah** prayed and said, My heart rejoiceth in the Lord, mine horn is exalted in the Lord; my mouth is enlarged over mine enemies: because I rejoice in thy salvation."

1165bc.

1 SAM. 2:21. "And the Lord visited **Hannah**, so that she conceiced, and bare three sons and two daughters. And the child Samuel grew before the Lord,"

HAZELELPONI

1300bc.

(342(1 CHRON. 4:3. "And these were of the father of Etam; Jezreel, and Ishma, and Idbash: and the name of their sister was **Hazelelponi.**"

HELAH

(342) 1 CHRON 4:5. And Ashur the father of Tekoa had two wives, **Helah** and Naarah."

1 CHRON. 4:7. "And the sons of **Helah** were Zereth, and Jezoar, and Ethnan."

HEPH-ZIBAH

698bc.

(334) 2 KINGS. 21:1 "Manasseh was twelve years old when he began to reign, and reigned fifty and five years in Jerusalem. And his mother's name was **Heph-zibah.**"

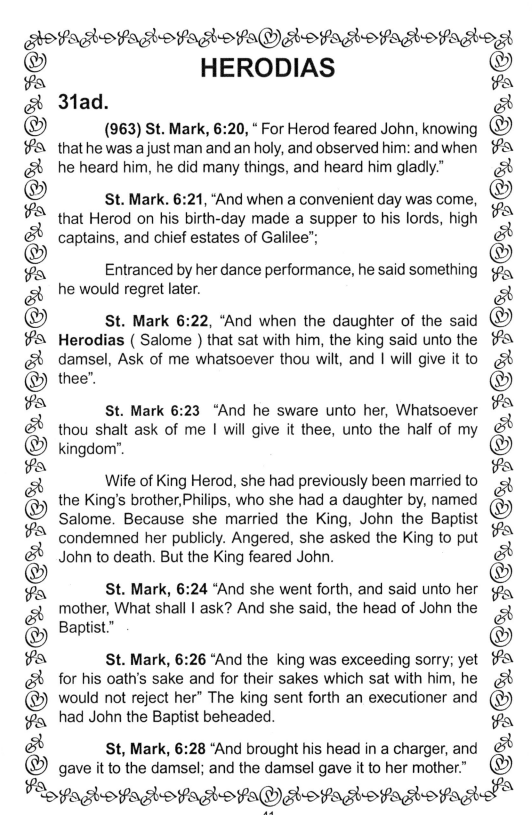

HERODIAS

31ad.

(963) St. Mark, 6:20, " For Herod feared John, knowing that he was a just man and an holy, and observed him: and when he heard him, he did many things, and heard him gladly."

St. Mark. 6:21, "And when a convenient day was come, that Herod on his birth-day made a supper to his lords, high captains, and chief estates of Galilee";

Entranced by her dance performance, he said something he would regret later.

St. Mark 6:22, "And when the daughter of the said **Herodias** (Salome) that sat with him, the king said unto the damsel, Ask of me whatsoever thou wilt, and I will give it to thee".

St. Mark 6:23 "And he sware unto her, Whatsoever thou shalt ask of me I will give it thee, unto the half of my kingdom".

Wife of King Herod, she had previously been married to the King's brother,Philips, who she had a daughter by, named Salome. Because she married the King, John the Baptist condemned her publicly. Angered, she asked the King to put John to death. But the King feared John.

St. Mark, 6:24 "And she went forth, and said unto her mother, What shall I ask? And she said, the head of John the Baptist."

St. Mark, 6:26 "And the king was exceeding sorry; yet for his oath's sake and for their sakes which sat with him, he would not reject her" The king sent forth an executioner and had John the Baptist beheaded.

St, Mark, 6:28 "And brought his head in a charger, and gave it to the damsel; and the damsel gave it to her mother."

HODESH

1400bc.

(346) 1 CHRON. 8:9. "And he begat of **Hodesh** his wife, Jobab, and Zibia, and Mesha, and Malcham."

HODIAH

1300bc.

(342) 1 CHRON. 4:19. "And the sons of his wife **Hodiah** the sister of Naham, the father of Keilah the Garmite, and Eshtemoa the Maachathite.

HOGLAH

1452bc

(143) NUM.26:33. "And Zelophehad the son of Hepher had no sons, but daughters: and the names of the daughters of Zelophehah, Mahlah, and Noah, **Hoglah**, Milcah, and Tirzah."

(144) NUM. 27:1. "Then came the daughters of Zelophehad, the son of Hepher, the son of Gilead, the son of Machir, the son of Manasseh, of the families of Manasseh the son of Joseph: and these are the names of his daughters; Mahlah, Noah, and **Hoglah**, and Milcah, and Tirzah."

1451bc.

(153) NUM. 36:11. "For Mahalah, Tirzah, and **Hoglah**, and Milcah, and Noah, the daughters of Zelophehad, were married unto their father's brothers' sons::

1444bc.

(204) JOSH.17:3 "And Zelophehad, the son of Hepher, the son of Gilead, the son of Machir, the son Manasseh, had no sons, but daughters,: and these are names of his daughters, Mahlah, and Noah, **Hoglah**, Milcah, and Tirzah."

HULDAH

624bc.

(335) 2 KINGS 22:14. "So Hilkiah the priest, and Ahikam, and Achbor, and Shaphan and Asahiah went unto **Huldah** the prophetess, the wife of Shallum the son of Tikvah, the son of Harhas, keeper of the wardrobe; and they communed with her"

(401) 2 CHRON. 34:22. "And Hilkiah, and they that the king had appointed, went to **Huldah** the prophetess, and the wife of Shallum the son of Tikvath......"

HUSHIM

1400BC.

(346) 1 CHRON. 8:8. "And Shaharim begat children in the country of Moab, after he had sent them away; **Hushim** and Baara were his wives."

1 CHRON. 8:11. "And **of Hushim** he begat Abitub and Elpaal."

ISCAH

2056bc.

(11) Gen. 11:29 "And Abram and Nahor took them wives: the name of Abram's wife was Sarai; and   the name of Nahor's wife Milcah, the daughter of Haran , the father of Milcah, and the father of **Iscah**".

JAEL

1296bc.

(215) JUD. 4:17. "Howbeit, Sisera fled away on his feet to the tent of **Jael** the wife of Heber the Kenite: for there was peace between Jabin the king of Hazor and the house of Heber the Kenite."

JUD. 4:18. "And **Jael** went out to meet Sisera, and said unto him, Turn in, my lord, turn in to me: fear not. And when he had turned in unto her into the tent, she covered him with a mantle."

JUD. 4:21. "Then **Jael** Heber's wife took a nail of the tent, and took a hammer in her hand, and went softly unto him, and smote the nail into his temple, and fastened it unto the ground: for he was asleep, and weary. So he died."

(216) JUD. 5:6. "In the days Shamgar the son of Anath, in the days of **Jael**, the highways were unoccupied, and the travelers walked through by-ways,"

JUD. 5:24. "Blessed above women shall **Jael** the wife of Heber the Kenite be, blessed shall she be above women in the tent."

JECHOLIAH

784bc.

(328) 2 KINGS. 15:1. "In the twenty and seventh year of Jeroboam king of Israel began Azariah son of Amaziah king of Judah to reign.

2 KINGS. 15:2. "Sixteen years old was he when he began to reign, and he reigned two and fifty years in Jerusalem. And his mother's name was **Jecholiah** of Jerusalem."

JEDIDAH

698bc.

(335) 2 KINGS. 22:1 "Josiah was eight years old when he began to reign, and he reigned thirty and one years in Jerusalel. And his mother's name was **Jedidah** the daughter of Adaiah of Boscath."

JEHOADDAN

839bc.

(327) 2 KINGS 14:2 "He was twenty and five years old when he began to reign, and reigned twenty and nine years in Jersualem . And his mother's name was **Jehoaddan** of Jersualem."

(392) 2 CHRON. 25:1 "Amaziah was twenty and five years old when he began to reign, and he reigned twenty and nine years in Jerusalem. And his mother's name was **Jehoaddan** of Jerusalem."

JEHOSHABEATH

Jehoshaheath and **Jehosheba** below are the same person, from two different books.

884bc.

(389) 2 CHRON. 22:11. "But **Jehoshabeath**, the daughter of the king, took Joesh the son of Ahaziah, and stole him from among the king's sons that were slain, and put him and his nurse in a bed-chamber. So **Jehoshabeath**, the **daughter of king Jehoram**, the wife of Jehoiada the priest, (for she was the sister of Ahaziah,) hid him from Athaliah, so that she slew him not.."

JEHOSHEBA

884bc.

(324) 2 KINGS.11:2. "But **Jehosheba**, the daughter of king Joram, sister of Ahaziah, took Joash the son of Ahaziah, and stole him from among the king's sons which were slain; and they hid him and his nurse, in the bed-chamber, from Athaliah, so that he was not slain."

JEHUDIJAH

1300bc.

(342) 1 CHRON. 4:18. "And his wife **Jehudijah** bare Jered the father of Gedor, and Heber the father of Socho, and Jekuthiel the father of Zanoah. And these are the sons of Bithiah the daughter of Pharaoh, which Mered took."

JEMIMA

1520bc.

(478) JOB. 42:14. "And he called the name of the first, **Jemima**; and the name of the second, Kezia; and the name of the third,Keren-happuch."

JERIOTH

1471bc.

(340) 1 CHRON. 2:18 "And Caleb the son Hezron begat children of Azubah his wife, and of **Jerioth**: her sons are these; Jesher, and Shobab, and Ardon."

JERUSHA

759bc.

(328) **2 KINGS.15:33.** "Five and twenty years old was he when he began to reign, and he reigned sixteen years in Jerusalem. And his mother's name was **Jerusha**, the daghter of Zadok."

758bc.

(394) **2 CHRON. 27:1.** Jotham was twenty and five years old when he began to reign, and he reign sixteen years in Jerusalem. His mother's name was **Jerusha**, the daghter of Zadok."

JEZEBEL

925bc.

(307) 1 KINGS 16:31 . "And it came to pass, as if it had a light thing for him to walk in the sins of Jeroboam the son Nebat, that he took to wife **Jezebel** the daughter of Ethbaal king of Zidoians, and went and served Baal, and worshipped him."

910bc.

(309) 1 KINGS 18:4 "For it was so, when **Jezebel** cut off the prophets of the Lord, that Obadiah took an hundred prophets , and hid them by fifty in a cave, and fed them with bread and water."

1 KINGS18:13 "Was it not told my lord what I did when **Jezebel** slew the prophets of the Lord, how I hid an hundred men of the Lord's prophets by fifty in a cave, and fed them with bread and water?"

1 KINGS 18:19 "Now therefore send, and gather to me all Israel unto mount Carmel, and the prophets of Baal four hundred and fifty, and the prophets of the groves four hundred, which eat at **Jezebel's** table."

906bc.

(310) 1 KINGS 19:1 "And Ahab told **Jezebel** all that Elijah had done, and withal how he had slain all the prophets with the sword."

900bc.

1 KINGS 19:2 "Then **Jezebel** sent to a messenger unto Elijah, saying, So let the gods do to me , and more also, if I make not of thy life as the life of one of them by tomorrow about this time."

899bc.

(312) **1 KINGS 21:5** "But **Jezebel** his wife came to him, and said, unto him, Why is thy spirit so sad, that thou eatest no bread ?"

1 KINGS 21:7 "And **Jezebel** his wife said unto him, Dost thou now govern the kingdom of Israel? arise, and eat bread and let thine heart be merry: I will give thee the vinyard of Naboth the Jezreelite."

1 KINGS 21:11 "And the menof the cit y, even the elders and the nobles who were the inhabitants in his city, did as **Jezebel** had sent unto them, and as it was written in the letters which she had sent unto them."

1 KINGS 21:14 "Then they sent to **Jezebel**, saying, Naboth is stoned, and is dead."

1 KINGS 21:15 "And it came to pass, when **Jezebel** heard that Naboth was stoned, and was dead, that **Jezebel** said to Ahab, Arise, take possession of the vineyard of Naboth, the Jezreelite, which he refused to give thee for money: for Naboth is not alive, but dead."

1 KINGS 21:23 "And of **Jezebel** also spake the Lord, saying, The dogs shall eat **Jezebel** by the wall of Jezreel."

1 KINGS 21;25 "But there was none like Ahab, which did sell himself to work wickedness in the sight of the Lord, whom **Jezebel** his wife stirred up."

884bc.

(322) **2 KINGS 9:7** "And thou shalt smite the house of Ahab thy master, that I may avenge the blood of my servants the prophets, and the blood of all the servants of the Lord, at the hand of **Jezebel**."

2 KINGS 9:10 "And the dogs shall eat **Jezebel** in the portion of Jezreel, and there shall be none to bury her."

2 KINGS 9:22 "And it came to pass, when Joram saw Jehu that he said, Is it pease Jehu? And he answerd, What peace, so long as the whoredoms of thy mother **Jezebel** and her witchcrafts are many?"

2 KINGS 9:30 "And when Jehu was come to Jezeel, **Jezebel** heard of it; and painted her face, and tired her head, and looked out the window."

2 KINGS 9:36 "Wherefore they came again, and told him. And he said, This is the word of the Lord, which he spake by his servent Elijah the Tishbite, saying, In the portion of Jezreel shall dogs eat flesh of **Jezebel**."

2 KINGS 9:37 "And the carcass of **Jezebel** shall be like dung upon the face of the field in the portion of Jezreel; so that they might not say, This is **Jezebel**."

JOANNA

31ad.

(981) **LUKE. 8:3.** "And **Joanna** the wife of Chuza, Herod's steward, and Susanna, and many others, which ministered unto him of their substance."

33ad.

(997) **LUKE.24:10,** "And it was Mary Magdalene, and **Joanna,** and Mary the mother of James and other women that were with them, which told these things unto the apostles."

JOCHEBED

Mother of Moses

1491bc.

(56) EXOD. 6:20. "And Amram took him **Jochebed** his father's sister to wife; and she bare him Aaron and Moses. And the years of Amram were an hundred and thirty and seven years".

(Compare these two books and the difference of 39 years.)

1452bc.

(143) NUM. 26:59. "And the name of Amram's wife was **Jochebed**, the daughter of Levi, whom her mother bare to Levi in Egypt: and she bare unto Amram, Aaron and Moses, and Miriam their sister."

JUDAH

612bc.

(748) JER. 3:7. "And I said after she had done all these things, Turn thou onto me. But she returned not. And her treacherous sister **Judah** saw it."

JER. 3:8 " And I saw, when for all the causes whereby backsliding Israel committed adultery, I had put her away, and given her a bill of divorce, yet her treacherous sister **Judah** feared not, but went and played the harlot also."

JER. 3:10. "And yet for all this, her treacherous sister **Judah** hath not turned unto me with her whole heart, but feignedly, saith the Lord."

JUDITH

1804bc.

(26) Gen, 26:34 "And Esau was forty years old when he took to wife **Judith** the daughter of Beeri the Hittite, and Bashemath the daughter of Elon the Hittite:"

When the town of Bethulia, where **Judith** lived, was under siege by the Asyrian army, their water supply had been cut off. Many of the people had decided to surrender. Unfaltering, **Judith** took it upon her self to save her people. Along with her maid and her trust in God, she set off for the enemy's camp. With her beguiling manner, she persuaded some Assyrian guards to take her to General Holoferrnes, the head of the army. She told Holofernes that the people of Bethulia had forsaken God and that God was about to punish them. She told him she had talked to God and God would tell her when this was to be. He believed her. They had dinner together and because he drank very heavily, it wasn't long before he fell asleep. She very carfully extracted his sword from its scabbard and, praying to God for strength, she chopped off his head. Consealing the head in a bag, she and her maid, made their way back to town. Returning home, she told the people what she had done. After they saw Holofernes' head, they gave up the idea of surrendering and, with renewed strength, and God on their side, they battled the Assyrians and won.

JULIA

60ad.

(1062) ROM. 16:15. "Salute Philologus, and **Julia**, Nereus, and his sister, and Olympas, and all the saints which are with them."

KEREN-HAPPUCH

1520bc.

(478) JOB 42:14. "And he called the name of the first, Jemima; and the name of the second,Kezia; and the name of the third, **Keren-happuch.**"

KETURAH

1853bc.

(25) GEN.25:1 "Then again Abraham took a wife, and her name was **Keturah.**"

Gen.25:4 "And the sons of Midian; Ephah, and Epher, and Hanoch, and Abidah, and Eldaah. All these were the sons of **Keturah.**"

(339) 1 CHRON. 1:32 "Now the sons of **Keturah** , Abraham's concubine: she bare Zimran, and Jokshan, and Midain, and Ishbak, and Shuah. And the sons Jokshan; Sheba, and Dedan."

1 CHRON. 1:33 "And the sons of Midian; Ephah, and Epher, and Henoch, and Abida, and Abida, and Eldaah. All these are the sons of **Keturah.**"

Note; In **Genesis**, Hanoch is spelled with an "A", In 1 **Chronicles** Henoch is spelled with an "E".

KEZIA

1520bc

(479) JOB 42:14. . "And he called the name of the first, Jemima; and the name of the second, **Kezia**; and the name of the third,Keren-happuch."

LEAH

1760bc

(29) Gen: 29:16 "And Laban had two daughters: the name of the elder was **Leah,** and the name of the younger was Rachel."

Her father, Laban, had given her sister, Rachel, to Jacob, the son of Rebekah, who was the daughter of her father's brother.

Gen. 29:17. "**Leah** was tender-eyed; but Rachel was beautiful and well-favoured."

Gen. 29:23 "And it came to pass in the evening, that he took **Leah** his daughter, and brought her to him; and he went in unto her".

Gen. 29:24 "And Laban gave unto his daughter **Leah,** Zilpah his maid, for an handmaid."

Gen. 29:25 "And it came to pass, that in the morning, behold, it was **Leah:** and he said to Laban, What is this thou hast done unto me? did not I serve with thee for Rachel? Wherefor then hast thou beguiled me?"

Gen. 29:30. "And he went in also unto Rachel, and he loved also Rachel more than **Leah,** and served with him yet seven other years."

Gen. 29:31. "And when the Lord saw that **Leah** was hated, he opened her womb: but Rachel was barren."

1752bc.

Gen. 29:32. "And **Leah** conceived, and bare a son, and she called his name Reuben: for she said, Surely the Lord hath looked upon my affliction; now therefore my husband will love me."

1739bc

Gen. 33:1. "And Jacob lifted up his eyes, and looked, and, behold, Esau came and with him four hundred men. And he devided the children unto **Leah,** and unto Rachel, and unto the two handmaids

(33) Gen. 33:2. "And he put the handmaides and their children foremost, and **Leah** and her children after, and Rachel and Joseph hindermost."

Gen. 33:7 "And **Leah** also with her children came near, and bowed themselves; and after came Joseph near and **Rachel**, and they bowed themselves."

1689bc.

(49) GEN. 49:31. "There they buried Abraham and Sarah his wife; there they buried Isaac and Rebekah his wife, and there I buried **Leah.**

1312bc.

(236) RUTH 4:11"And all the people that were in the gate, and the elders, said, We are witnesses. The Lord make the woman that is come into thine house like Rachel and like **Leah,** which two did build the house of Israel: and do thou worthily in Ephratah and be famous in Bethlehem."

LILITH
(The First Woman)
Hebrew Bible:

3761bc.

She is found in Jewish literature where it is said that she was Adams' first wife.

A contradiction in that the Hebrew Bible has her born 243 years after Eve was born .

God had decided to create a companion for Adam. He created her in the same manner that He created Adam, out of earth.

She and Adam argued right from the start because she would not do Adams' bidding. Because of this she was expelled from the Garden of Eden. She had, however, slept with Adam and gave birth to "evil spirits".

Adam called upon God to bring her back. But she refused.

God sent three angels after her. Still she refused to go back to Adam and vowed she would harm newborn children, male and female alike.

She became a succubus, "a demon who gave birth of witches." An incubus having intercourse with men while they slept.

Some Jewish historians believe she is mentioned in **Isaiah 34:14,** where she is said to be the "screech-owl".

In other writings, she is referred to as a "night hag" and an enemy of newborn children.

She is also found in Babylonian myth.

She was said to of been married to Satan.

Others say she was the wife of Samael, Angel of Death.

LO-RUHAMAH

785bc.

(863) HOS. 1:6. "And she conceived again, and bare a daughter. And God said unto him, Call her name LO-ruhamah."

HOS.1:8. "Now when she had weaned Lo-ruhamah, she conceived and bare a Son".

LOTS' WIFE

Lot was the brother of Abraham who was the forefather of the Hebrew people. When Lot was a resident of Sodom, he was warned by angels of the imminent destruction of the city.

1898bc.

(19) Gen: 19:24 " Then the Lord rained upon Sodom and upon Gomorrh brimstone and fire from the Lord out of heaven".

As they fled the city, God told them not to look back.

Gen: 19:26 "But his wife looked back from behind him, and she became a Pillar of salt".

LYDIA

53ad.

(1034) ACTS. 16:14. "And a certain woman named **Lydia**, a seller of purple, of the city of Thyatira, which worshipped God, heard us: whose heart the Lord opened, that she attended unto the things which were spoken of Paul."

ACTS. 16:40. "And they went out of the prison, and entered into the house of **Lydia**: and when they had seen the brethren, they comforted them and departed."

MAACHAH

1872bc.

(22) GEN. 22:24 "And his concubine, whose name was Reumah, she bare alsoTebah, and Gaham , and Thahash, and **Maachah**."

MAACHAH 2

1471bc.

(340) 1 CHRON. 2:48 "**Maachah**, Caleb'a concubine, bare Sheber, and Tiranah."

1 CHRON. 2:49 "She bare also Shaaph the father of Madmannah, Sheva the father of Machbenah, and the father of Gibea: and the daughter of Caleb was Achsah"

(341) 1 CHRON. 3:2. "The third, Absalon the son of **Maachah** the daughter of Tahmai king of Geshur: the fourth, Adonijah the son of Haggith:"

MAACHAH 3

Wife of Machir

1444bc.

(345) 1 CHRON. 7:15. "And Machir took to wife the sister of Huppim and Shuppim, whose sister's name was **Maachah**; and the name of the second was Zelophehad: and Zelophehad had daughters."

1 CHRON. 7:16. "And **Maacha**h the wife of Machir bare a son and she called his name Peresh; and the name of his brother was Sheresh; and his sons were Ulam, and Rakem."

(346) 1 Chron. 8:29. "And at Gibeon dwelt the father of Gibeon whose wife's name was **Maachah**."

MAACHAH 4

Mother of Absalon

1053bc.

(270) 2 Sam. 3:3 "And his second, Chileab, of Abigail the wife of Nabal the Carmelite, and the third, Absalon the son of **Maachah**, the daughter of Talmai king of Geshur;

MAACHAH 5

Mother of Shelomith

974bc.

(378) **2 Chron. 11:20.** "And after **Maachah,** the daughter of Abhsalom; which bare him Abijah, And Attai, and Zisa, and Shelomith."

2 Chron. 11:21. "And Rehoboam loved **Maachah** the daughter of Absalom above all his wives and his concubines: (for he took eighteen wives, and threescore concubines; and begat twenty and eight sons, and three-score daughters.)"

2 Chron. 11:22. "And Rehoboam made Alijah the son of **Maachah** the chief, to be ruler amomg his brethern: for he thought to make him king."

MAACHAH 6

Mother of Abijam

1200bc.

(347) **1 Chron. 9:35.** "And Gibeon dwelt the father of Gibeon, Jehiel, whose wife's name was **Maachah."**

958bc.

(328) **1 KINGS 15:1** "Now in the eighteenth year of king Jeroboam the son of Nebat reigned Abijam over Juda.

1 Kings 15:2. "Three years he reigned in Jerusalem. And his mother's name was **Maachah**, the daughter of Abishalom."

955bc.

(328) **1 Kings 15:10.** "And fourty and one years reigned he in Jerusalem. And his mother's name was **Maachah**, the daughter of Abishalom."

1 Kings 15:13. "And also **Maachah** his mother, even her he removed from being queen, because she had made an idol in a grove; an Asa destroyed her idol, and burnt it by the brook Kidron."

941bc.

(382) **2 Chron. 15:16.** "And also concerning **Maachah** the mother of Asa the king, he removed her from being queen, because she had made an idol in a grove; and Asa cut down her idol, and stamped it, and burnt it at the brook Kidron."

MAHALAH

1444bc.

(345) 1 CHRON. 7:18. "And his sister Hammoleketh bare Ishod. And Abiezer, and **Mahalah**.

MAHALATH

Wife of Esae.

1760bc.

(28) GEN.28;9. "Then went Esae unto Ishmael, and took unto the wives which he had **Mahalath** the daughter of Ishmael Abraham's son, the sister of Nebajoth, to be his wife.'"

MAHALATH 2

974bc.

(378) 2 CHRON. 11:18. "And Rehoboam took him **Mahalath** the daughter of Jerimoth the son of David to wife, and Abihail the daughter Eliab the son of Jese;'

MAHLAH

NUM. 26:33 And Zelophehad the son of Helper had no sons, but daughter: and the names of the daughters of Zelophehad **MAHLAH** , Noah, Hoglah, Milcah and Tirzah**1452bc.**

(143) NUM. 26:33. "And Zelophehad the son of Hepher had no sons, but daughters: and the names of the daughters of Zelophehad were Mahlah, and Noah, **Hoglah**, Milcah, and Tirzah."

(1444) NUM. 27:1. "Then came the daughters of Zelophehad, the son of Hepher, the son of Gilead, the son of Machir, the son of Manasseh, of the families of Manasseh the son of Joseph: and these are the names of his daughters; **Mahlah**, Noah, and Hoglah, and Milcah, and Tirzah."

1444bc.

(204) JOSH. 17:3 "But Zelophehad, the son of Hepher, the son of Gilead, the son of Machir, the son Manasseh, had no sons, but daughters,: and these are names of his daughters, **Mahlah**, and Noah, Hoglah, Milcah, and Tirzah."

MARA

1312bc.

(233) RUTH. 1:20. "And she said unto them, Call me not Naomi, call me **Mara:** for the Allmighty hath dealt very bitterly with me."

MARTHA

33ad.

(1008) John 11:1 "Now a certain man was sick, named Lazarus, of Bethany, the town of Mary and her sister **Martha.**"

John 11:2 "(It was Mary which anointed the Lord with ointment, and wiped his feet with her hair, whose brother Lazarus was sick.)"

John 11:3 "Therefor his sisters sent unto him, saying, Lord, behold, he whom thou lovest is sick."

John 11:4 "When Jesus heard that , he said, "This sickness is not unto death, but for the glory of God, that the Son of God might be glorified thereby".

John 11:5 "Now Jesus loved **Martha**, and her sister, and Lazarus". But Jesus stayed away for two days before going to them.

John 11:21 "Then said **Martha** unto Jesus, Lord, if thou hadst been here, my brother had not died". His body was placed in a tomb.

John 11:22 "But I know that even now, whatsoever thou wilt ask of God, God will give it thee". Then Jesus told her that her brother shall rise again.

John 11:26 "And whosoever liveth and believeth in me, shall never die. Believest thou this?

John 11:39 "Jesus said take away the stone. **Martha**, the sister of him that was dead, saith unto him, Lord, by this time he stinketh: for he hath been dead for four days". They rolled back the stone from the tomb and Lazarus came out into the light".

MARY MAGDALENE

31ad.

A close friend of Martha and Mary of Bethany and, like Mary, she, to, washed the feet of Jesus.

(980) Luke 7:38 "And stood at his feet behind him weeping, and began to wash his feet with tears, and did wipe them with the hairs of her head, and kissed his feet and anointed them with the ointment."

LUKE 7:39 "Now when the Pharises, which had hidden him, saw it, he spake within himself' saying, This man, if he were a prophet, would have known who, and what manner of woman this is that toucheth him: for she is a sinner."

Luke 7:44 "And he turned to the woman, and he said unto Simon, "Seest thou this woman? I entered into thine house, thou gavest me no water for my feet: But she has washed my feet with tears, and wiped them with the hairs of her head."

Jesus continued to scold Simon by telling him that he given no water for his feet. That the woman had washed his feet with tears and had wiped dry with the hairs of her head. When I entered your house, you gave me no kiss, Yet this woman has not ceased to kiss my feet. You did not anoint my head with oil but this woman has anointed my feet with oil.

Luke 7:47 "Wherefore, I say unto thee, Her sins which are many, are forgiven; for she loved much: but to whom little is forgiven, the same loveth little."

Luke 7:48 "And I said unto her, Thy sins are forgiven." She was healed of evil spirits:

LUKE 7:50 "And he said to the woman, Thy faith hath saved thee; go in peace."

(981) Luke, 8:2 "And certain women which had been healed of evil spirits and imfirmities, **Mary** called **Magdalene**, out of whom went seven devils."

33ad.

(1009) John, 12:3 "Then took **Mary** a pound of ointment of spikenard, very costly, and anointed the feet of Jesus, and wiped his feet with her hair and the house was filled with the odour of the ointment."

She was at the crufixion of Jesus.

(956) Matth. 27:55 "And many women were there (beholding afar off) which followed Jesus from Galilee, ministering unto him:"

Matth. 27:56 "Among which was **Mary Magdalene**, and Mary the mother of James and Joses, and the mother of Zebedee's children."

She was one of the first to learn of the resurrection.

(973) Mark 16:1 "And when the Sabbath was past, **Mary Magdalene**, and Mary the mother of James, and Salome, had bought sweet spices, that they might come and anoint him."

MARY, MOTHER OF JESUS

**The Fifth Year
before the Common
Acount called
Anno Domini.**

In the town of Nazareth was a young virgin, named **Mary,** who was betrothed to a carpenter named Joseph. One day an angel came to her;

(930) Mathew 1:18 "Now the birth of Jesus Christ was on this wise: When as his mother **Mary** was espoused to Joseph, before they came together, she was found with child of the Holy Ghost".

Mathew 1:19 "Then Joseph her husband, being a just man, and not willing to make her a public example, was minded to put her away privily".

Mathew 1:20 "But while he thought on these things, behold, the angel of the Lord appeared unto him in a dream, saying, Joseph, thou son of David, fear not to take unto thee **Mary** thy wife: for that which is conceived in her is of the Holy Ghost".

Mathew 1:23 "Behold, a virgin shall be with child, and shall bring forth a son, and, they shall call his name Emanuel, which being interpreted is, God with us.)"

Mathew 1:24 "Then Joseph, being raised from sleep, did as the angel of the Lord had bidden him, and took unto him his wife":

Mathew 1:25 "And knew her not till she had brought forth her first-born son: and he called his name Jesus."

(974) Luke 1:27 "To a virgin espoused to a man whose name was Joseph, of the house of David; and the virgin's name was **Mary."**

Luke 1:30 "And the angel said unto her, Fear not, **Mary:** for thou hast found favour with God."

Luke 1:31 " And behold, thou shalt conceive in thy womb, and bring forth a son, and shalt call his name Jesus."

Luke 1:33 "And he shall reign over the house of Jacob for ever; and of his kingdom there shall be no end."

Luke 1:34 " Then said **Mary** unto the angel, How shall this be. I know not a man?."

Luke 1:35 "And the angel answered and said ento her, The Holy Ghost shall overshadow thee: therefore also that holy thing which shall be born of thee, shall be called the Son of God."

Luke 1:38 "And **Mary** said, Behold the handmaid of the Lord, be it unto me according to thy word. And the angel departed from her."

Luke 1:39 "And **Mary** arose in those days, and went into the hill-country with haste, into the city of Juda."

Luke 1:46 "And **Mary** said, My soul doth magnify the Lord."

MATRED

1496bc.

(36) GEN.36:39. "And Baal-hanan the son of Achbor died, and Hadar reigned in his stead: and the name of the his city was Pau; and his wife's name was Mehetabel, the daughterof **Matred,** the daughter of Mezahab."

(339) 1 CHRON. 1:50 "And when Baal-hanan was dead , Hadad reigned in his stead: and the name of his city was Pai; and his wife's name was Mehetabel, the daughter of **Matred,** the daughter of Mezahab."

Note: The name of "his" city is spelled differently, Pau and Pai, both are correct.

MEHETABEL

1496bc.

(36) GEN. 36:39 "An Baal-hanan the son of Achbor died,and Hadar reigned in his stead: and the name of the his city was Pau; and his wife's was **Mehetabel,** the doughter of Matred, the daughter of Mezahab."

(339) 1 CHRON. 1:50 "And when Baal-hanan was dead , Hadad reigned in his stead: and the name of his city was Pai; and his wif's name was **Mehetabel,** the daughter of Matred, the daughter of Mezahab."

MERAB

1087bc

(250) 1 SAM. 14:49. "Now the sons of Saul were Jonathan, and Ishui, and Melchi-shua: and the names of his two daughters were these; the name first-born **Merab**, and the name of the younger Michal."

1063bc.

(254) 1 SAM. 18:17. "And Saul said to David, Behold, my elder daughter **Merab**, her will I give to thee to wife: only be thou valiant to me, and fight the Lords battles. For Saul said, Let not mine hand be upon him, but let the hand of the Philistines be upon him.

1 SAM. 18:19. "But it came to pass at a time when **Merab**, Saul's daughter, should have been given to David, that she was given unto Adriel the Meholathite to wife."

MESHULLEMETH

643bc.

(334) 2 KINGS 21:19. "Amon was twenty and two years old when he began to reign, and he reigned two years in Jerusalem. And his mother's name was **Meshullemeth**."

MICHAIAH

958bc.

(380) 2 CHRON. 13:2. "He reigned three years in Jerusalem.His mother's name also **Michaiah** the daughter of Uriel of Gibeah."

MICHAL

1087bc.

(250) 1 SAM. 14:49. "Now the sons of Saul were Jonathan, and Ishui, and Melchi-shua: and the names of his two daughters were these; the name first-born Merab, and the name of the younger **Michal**."

1063bc.

(254) 1 SAM.18:20. "And **Michal**, Saul's daughter, loved David: and they told Saul, and the thing pleased him."

1 SAM. 18:27. "Wherefore David arose and went, he and his men, slew of the Phlistines two hundred men; and David brought their foreskins, and they gave them in full tale to the king, that he might be the king's son-in-law. And Saul gave him **Michal** his daughter to wife."

1 SAM. 18:28. "And Saul saw and knew that the Lord was with David, and that **Michal**, Saul's daughter, loved him."

1062bc.

(255) 1 SAM. 19:11. "Saul also sent messengers unto David's house, to watch him, and to slay him in the morning: and **Michal**, David's wife, told him, saying, If thou save not thy life to-night, tomorrow thou shalt be slain."

1 SAM. 19:12. "So **Michal** let David down through a window: and he went and fled, and escaped."

1 SAM. 19:13. "And **Michal** took an image, and laid it in the bed, and put a pillow of goats' hair for his bolster, and covered it with a cloth."

1 SAM. 19:17. "And Saul said unto **Michal**, 'Why hast thou deceived me so, and sent away mine enemy, that he is escaped'? And **Michal** answered Saul, He said unto me , let me go; why should I kill thee."

1060bc.

(261) 1 SAM. 25:44. "But Saul had given **Michal** his daughter, David's wife, to Phalti the son of Laish, which was of Galim."

1048bc.

(239) 2 SAM. 3:13. "And he said, Well; I will make a league with thee: but one thing I require of thee, that is, Thou shalt not see my face , except thou first bring **Michal**, Saul's daughter, when thou comest to see my face."

2 SAM. 3:14. "And David sent messengers to Ish-bosheth, Saul's son, saying , Deliver me my wife **Michal**, which I espoused to me, for an hundred foreskins of the Philistines."

1042bc.

(253) 1 CHRON. 15:29 "And it came to pass, as the ark of the covenant of the Lord came to the city of David, that **Michal** the daughter of Saul looking out at a window saw King David dancing and playing: and she despised him in her heart."

1452bc.

(143) NUM. 26:33. "And Zelophehad the son of Hepher had no sons, but daughters: and the names of the daughters of Zelophehad were Mahlah, and Noah, Hoglah, Milcah, and **Tirzah**."

(1444) NUM. 27:1. "Then came the daughters of Zelophehad, the son of Hepher, the son of Gilead, the son of Machir, the son of Manasseh, of the families of Manasseh the son of Joseph: and these are the names of his daughters; Mahlah, Noah, and Hoglah, and Milcah, and **Tirzah**."

(153) NUM. 36:11. "For Mahalah, **Tirzah,** and Hoglah, and Milcah, and Noah, the daughters of Zelophehad, were married unto their father's brothers' sons:"

1444bc.

(204) JOSH. 17:3 "But Zelophehad, the son of Hepher, the son of Gilead, the son of Machir, the son Manasseh, had no sons, but daughters,: and these are names of his daughters, Mahlah, and Noah, Hoglah, Milcah, and **Tirzah**."

MILCAH

Nabors' wife.

1996bc.

(11) GEN. 11:29. "And Abram and Nahor took them wives: the name of Abram's wife was Sarai; and the name of Nahor's wife **Milcah**, the daughter of Haran, the father of Micah, and the father of Iscah."

1872bc.

(22) GEN. 22:20. "And it came to pass after these things, that it was told Abraham, saying, Behold, **Milcah**, she hath also born children unto thy brother Nahoh."

GEN. 22:,23. "And Bethuel begat Rebekah: these eight **Milcah** did bear to Nahor, Abraham's brother."

1857bc.

(24) GEN. 24:15. "And it came to pass, before he had done speaking, that, behold Rebekah came came out, who was born to Bethuel, son of **Milcah**, wife of Nahor, Abraham's brother, with her pitcher upon her shoulder."

GEN. 24:24. "And she said unto him, I am the daughter of Bethuel the son of **Milcah**, which she bare unto Nahor."

GEN. 24:47. "And I asked her, and said, Whose daughter art thou? And she said, the daughter of Bethuel, Nahor's son, which **Milcah** bare unto him: and I put the ear-ring upon her face, and the bracelets upon her hands."

MILCAH 2

Daughter of Zelophehad.

1452bc.

(143) **NUM. 26:33.** "And Zelophehad the son of Hepher had no sons, but daughters: and the names of the daughters of Zelophehah were Mahlah, and Noah, Hoglah, **Milcah**, and Tirzah."

(144) **NUM. 27:1.** "then came the daughters of Zelophehad, the son of Hepher, the son of Gilead, the son of Machir, the son of Manasseh, of the families of Manasseh the son of Joseph: and these are the names of his daughters; Mahlah, Noah, and Hoglah, and **Milcah**, and Tirzah."

1451bc.

(153) **NUM. 36:11.** "For Mahalah, Tirzah, and Hoglah, and **Milcah**, and Noah, the daughters of Zelophehad, were married unto their father's brothers' sons:"

1444bc.

(204) **JOSH. 17:3.** "But Zelophehad, the son of Hepher, the son of Gilead, the son of Machir, the son Manasseh, had no sons, but daughter,: and these are names of his daughters, Mahlah, and Noah, Hoglah, **Milcah**, and Tizah."

MIRIAM
Sister of Moses

1491bc.

"**Miriarm** was born fifteen years before Moses."
The story of M0SES begins:

(143) **Num. 26:59** "And the name of Amram's wife was Jochebed, the daughter of Levi, whom her mother bare to Levi in Egypt: and she bare unto Amram, Aaron and Moses, and **Miriam** their sister."

1706

(51) **Exod. 1:15** And the king of Egypt spake to the Hebrew midwives…"

Exod. 1:16 And he said, When you do the office of a midwife to the Hebrew women, and see them upon the stools; if it be a son, then ye shall kill him; ……."

To save her child, Moses's mother, Jochebed, placed him in a basket made of papyrus and set it floating on the river in the view of his sister, **Miriam** He was rescued by the daughter of Pharaoh, who brought the infant up as her own child.

One must question, where was Amram, the father of Moses?

1571 bc.

EXOD. 2:4. "And the sister stood afar off, to wit what would be done to him"

From the book of Jasher

About
2433 AM. Anno Mundi.
i.e, year of the world.

Same as 1571bc

The decree coming forth, that the Hebrew males should all be slain as they were born.

Miriam, having heard how good-natured the daughter of Pharoh was, proposed to her parents, that she would carry her brother Moses and meet the princess as she walked by the river side. Which was the custom of the princess every morning to do, and seem as though she was going to drown the infant."

"Then will I answar, and say I am going to drown it, it being an infant male of the children of Jacob, according to the decree of Pharaoh, thy father, which says, Every male that openeth the womb, amoung the children of Jacob, shall ye drown in the river."

"O, says Jochebed, thou art as a sea of bitterness unto me! O my daughter, thou hast ingulphed me in an ocean of perplexity! "

"Be not afraid, says **Miriam**, whether it is not all one, that he perish by the hands and command of the daughter of Pharaoh, or by the slayers of infants; we cannot always hide him from knowledge."

Miriam, almost by force, takes up the infant, and away she carries him to the banks of the river, to meet the princess.

Jochebed and Amram (the father of Moses) follow at some distance, waiting the event.

Now **Miriam** had placed herself under a tree, where she knew the princess would pass bay, and was there kissing, and taking, as it were, her last farewell of her brother, and as the princess approached, was swaddling it up, that with the greater convenience she might throw it into the river, and then kisses it again, and the tears flowed from her eyes.

The princess was taking her morning walk, attended by her women.

The princess and the ladies stood at some distance, viewing and thinking what the meaning of this thing could be; and seeing that the young woman looked at the water, and at the child, imagined that she was going to drown it . Upon this, the princess calls earnestly to **Miriam,** and asked her, what she was going to do with the infant?

Miriam advances, and says, I am about to drown it, even as Pharaoh has commanded.

How! Says the Princess, sure Pharaoh has not said it.

Then answered **Miriam,** Thy father hath said, "Every male that openeth the womb, among the children of Jacob, shall ye drown in the river."

And the princess said, "Give me the child."

Miriam having delivered the child, the princess enquires for one to nurse it.

Here **Miriam** produces her mother, Jochebad, to be a nurse for her brother.

Then Jochebed took Moses, and returned unto her house.

Thus did **Miriam,** when fifteen years of age, contrive the revoking of the decree of Pharoh.

Miriam from hence became the admired of the Hebrews.

Miriam was ninety-five years of age when Moses came from Midian.

MIRIAM 2

Daughterof Ezra.

1300bc.

(342) 1 CHRON. 4:17 "And the sons of Ezra were Jether. And Mered, and Epher, and Jalon: and she bare **Miriam**, and Shammai, and Ishbah the father of Eshtemoa."

NAAMAH

Daughter of Zillah.

3875bc.

(4) GEN.4:22. "And Zillah, she also bare Tubal-cain, an instructor of every artificer in brass and iron: and the sister of Tubal-cain was **Naamah**."

NAAMAH 2

Solomon's granddaughter.

971bc.

(379) 2 CHRON. 12:13. "So king Rehoboam strengthened himself in Jerusalem, and reigned: for Rehoboam was one and forty years old when he began to reign, and he reigned seventeen years in Jeruslem, the city which the Lord had chosen out of all the tribes of Israel, to put his name there. And his mother's name was **Naamah** an Ammomitess."

958bc.

(305) 1 KINGS 14:31. "And Rehoboam slept with his fathers, and was buried with his fathers in the city of David. And his mother's name was **Naamah** an Ammonitess. And Abijam his son reigned in his stead."

954bc,

1 KINGS 14: 21 "And Rehoboam the son of Solomon reigned in Judah. Rehoboam was forty and one years old when he began to reign; and he reign seventeen years in Jerusalem, the city which the Lord did choose out all the tribes of Israel, to put his name there: and his mother's name was **Naamah** an Ammonitess."

NAARAH

1300bc.

(342) 1 CHRON. 4:5. "And Ashur the father of Tekoa had two wives, Helah and **Naarah**".

1 CHRON. 4:6 "And **Naarah** bare Ahuzam, and Hepher, and Temeni, and Haahashtari. These were the sons of **Naarah**".

NAOMI

1322bc.

(233) **Ruth 1:3** "And Elimelech **Naomi's** husband died; and she was left, and her two sons."

The two sons married two women from Moab. One was named Ruth and the other Orpah. They dwelled in Moab for about ten years. Then Mahlon and Chilion died.

1312bc.

Ruth I:7 "Wherefore she went forth out of the place where she was, and her two daughters-in-law with her; and they went on the way to return unto the land of Juda".

Ruth 1:11 "And **Naomi** said, Turn again, my daughters: why will ye go with me? Are there any more sons in my womb, that may be your husbands?"

Naomi was married to Elimelech and they had two sons, Mahlon and Chilion.

Ruth 1:19 "So the two went until they came to Bethlehm. And it came to pass, when they were come to Beth-lehem, that all the city was moved about them, and said "*is* this **Naomi**?"

Ruth1:20 "And she said unto them, Call me not **Naomi**, call me Mara: for the Almighty hath dealt very bitterly with me".

NEHUSHTA

599bc.

(337) **2 KINGS 24:8.** "Jehoiachin was eighteen years old when he began to reign, and he reigned in Jerusalem three months. And his mother's name was **Nehushta**, the daughter of Elnathan of Jeruaslem."

NOADIAH

445bc.

(419) NEH. 6:14. "My God, think thou upon Tobith and Sanballat , according to these their works, and on the prophetess **Noadiah,** and the rest of the prophets, that would have put me in fear."

NOAH

1452bc.

(143) NUM. 26:33 "And Zelophehad the son of Hepher had no sons, but daughters: and the names of the daughters of Zelophehad Mahlah, and **Noah,** Hoglah, Milcah, and Tirzah."

(144) NUM. 27:1 "then came the daughters of Zelophehad, the son of Hepher, the son of Gilead, the son of Machir, the son of Manasseh, of the families of Manasseh the son of Joseph: and these are the names of his daughters; Mahlah, **Noah**, and Hoglah, and Milcah, and Tirzah."

(153) NUM. 36:11 "For Mahlah, Tirzah, and Hoglah, and Milcah, and **Noah,** the daughters of Zelophehad, were married unto their father's brothers' sons:"

1444bc.

(204) JOSH. 17:3 "But Zelophehad, the son of Hepher, the son of Gilead, the son of Machir, the son Manasseh, had no sons, but daughters,: and these are the names of his daughters, Mahlah, and **Noah**, Hoglah, Milcah, and Tircah."

NOAH'S WIFE

2448bc.

(6) **GEN. 6:18** "But with thee will I establish my covenant: and thou shalt come into the ark, thou, and thy sons, and thy **wife**, and thy sons' wives with thee."

2349bc. Time frame discrepancy, 99 years.

(7) **GEN. 7:7** "And Noah went in, and his sons, and his **wife**, and his sons wives with him, into the ark, because of the waters of the flood."

GEN.7:13. "In the self-same day entered Noah, and Shem, and Ham, and Japheth, the sons of Noah, and Noah's **wife**, and the three wives of his sons with them,into the ark:"

2348bc.

(8) **GEN. 8:16**. "Go forth of the ark, thou, and thy **wife**, and thy son, and thy sons wives with thee."

GEN. 8:18 "And Noah went forth, and his **wife**, and his sons'wives with him."

ORPAH

Sister of Ruth. Married to one of Naomi's two sons'.

1312bc.

(233) **1:14 Ruth** "And they lifted up their voice, and wept again. And **Orpah** kissed her mother-in-law; but Ruth clave unto her"

PENINAH

1171bc.

(237) 1 SAM.1:2. "And he had two wives; the name of the one was Hannah, and the name of the other was **Peninah:** and **Peninah** had children, but Hannah had no children."

1 SAM.1:4. "And when the time was that Elkanah offered, he gave to **Peninah** his wife, and to all her sons and her daughters, portions:"

PERSIS

60ad.

(1062) ROM. 16:12. "Salute Tryphena and Tryphosa, who labour in the Lord. Salute the beloved **Persis** which laboured much in the Lord."

PHANUEL

Before the account
called Anno Domini
the fourth year.

(975) LUKE.2:36 "And there was one Anna, a prophetese, the daughter of **Phanuel**, of the tribe of Aser: she was of great age , and had lived with an Husband seven years from her virginity."

PHEBE

60ad.

(1062) ROM. 16:1. "I commend unto you **Phebe** our sister, which is a servent of the church which is at Cenchrea:"

PILATE'S WIFE

33ad.

(956) MATT. 27:19. "When he was set down on the judgment, his wife sent unto him saying, Have thou nothing to do with that just man: for I have suffered many things this day in a dream, because of him."

PRISCILLA

54ad.

(1036) ACTS. 18:2 "And found a certain Jew named Aquila, born in Pontus, lately come from Italy, when his wife **Priscilla,** (because Claudius had commanded all Jews to depart from Rome) and come unto them."

55ad.

ACTS. 18:18 "And Paul after this tarried there yet a good while, and then took his leave of the brethren, and sailed thence into Syria, and with him **Priscilla**, and Aquila; having shorn his head in Cenctrea: for he had a vow."

ACTS. 18:26 "And he began to speak boldly in the synagogue: whom, when Aquila and **Priscilla** had heard, they took him unto them, and expounded unto him the way of God more perfectly."

PRISCA

Another name for Priscilla

66ad.

(1129) 2 TIM. 4:19 "Salute **Prisca** and Aquila, and the household of Onesiphorus."

PUAH

1635bc.

(51) **EXOD. 1:15.** " And the king of Egypt spake to the Hebrew midwives of which the name of one was Shiphrah, and the name of the other **Puah**;"

PUTIEL

1491bc.

(56) **EXOD. 6:25.** "And Eleazar, Aaron's son, took him one of the daughters of **Putiel** to wife; and she bare him Phinehas: these are the heads of the fathers of the Levites, according to their families."

RACHAB

Wife of Solomon.

The Fifth Year Before the Common Account called Ano Domini.

(930) **MATT. 1:5.** "And Salmon begat Booz of **Rachab**; and Booz begat Obed of Ruth; and Obed begat Jesse."

RACHEL

1760bc.

(29) GEN. 29:6 "And he said unto them, is he well?' And they said. He is well: and: behold, **Rachel** his daughter cometh with the sheep."

Gen. 29:9. "And while he yet spake with them, **Rachel** came with her father's sheep: for she kept them."

Gen. 29:10. "And it came to pass, when Jacob saw **Rachel** the daughter of Laban his mother's brother, and the sheep of Laban his mother's brother, that Jacob went near, and rolled the stone from the well's mouth, and watered the flock of Laban his mother's brother."

Gen. 29:11. "And Jacob kissed **Rachel,** and lifted up his voice, and wept."

Gen. 29:12, "And Jacob told **Rachel** that he was her father's brother, and that he was Rebekah's son; and she ran and told her father."

Gen: 29:16 "And Laban had two daughters: the name of the elder was Leah, and the name of the younger was **Rachel**.

Gen. 29:17. "Leah was tender-eyed; but **Rachel** was beautiful and well-favoured."

Gen. 29:18. "And Jacob loved **Rachel;** and said, I will serve thee seven years for Rachel thy younger daughter."

Gen. 29:20. "And Jacob served seven years for **Rachel;** and they seemed unto him but a fewv days, for the love he had to her."

1753bc.

Gen. 29:25 "And it came to pass, that in the morning, behold, it was Leah: and he said to Laban, What is this thou hast done unto me? did not I serve withthee for **Rachel**? Wherefor then hast thou beguiled me?"

Gen. 29:28. "And Jacob did so, and fulfilled her week: and he gave him Rachel his daughter to wed also.

Gen. 29:29. "And Laban gave to **Rachel** his daughter, Bilhah his handmaid, to be her maid."

Gen. 29:30. "And he went in also unto **Rachel,** and he loved also **Rachel** more than Leah, and served with him yet seven other years."

Gen. 29:31. "And when the Lord saw that Leah was hated, he opened her womb: but **Rachel** was barren."

1749bc.

(30) Gen. 30:6. And **Rachel** said, God hath judged me, and hath also heard my voice, and hath ginen me a son: therefore called she his name Dan."

1747bc.

Gen. 30:8. And **Rachel** said, With great wrestlings have I wrestled with my sister, and I have prevailed: and she called his name Naphtali."

1747bc.

Gen. 30:14. "And Reuben went in the days of wheat-harvest, and found mandrakes in the field and brought them unto his mother Leah. Then **Rachel** said to Leah, Give me, I pray thee, of my son's mandrakes."

1748bc.

Gen. 30;15. And she said unto her, Is it a small matter that thou hast taken my husband? And wouldest thou take away my son's mandrakes also? And **Rachel** said, Therefore he shal lie with thee to-night for thy son's mandrakes."

1745bc.

Gen. 30:22. "An God remembered **Rachel** and God harkened to her and opened her womb."

Gen. 30:25. "And it came to pass, when **Rachel** had born to Joseph, that Jacob said unto to Laban, Send me away, that I may go into mine own place, and to my own country."

1739bc

(31) Gen.31:4. "And Jacob sent and called **Rachel** and Leah to the field unto his flock."

Gen. 31:14. "And **Rachel** and Leah answered, and said unto him, Is there any portion or inheritance for us in our father's house?"

Gen. 31:19. "And Laban went to shear his sheep: and **Rachel** had stolen the images that were her father's."

Gen. 31:32. "With whomsoever thou findest thy gods, let him not live; before our brethren discern thou what is thine with me, and take it to thee. For Jacob knew not that **Rachel** had stolen them."

Gen. 31:33. "And Laban went into Jacob's tent, and into Leah's tent, and into the two maid-servants' tents; but he found them not. Then went he out of Leah's tent, and entered into **Rachel's** tent."

Gen. 31:34 "Now **Rachel** had taken the emages, and put them in the camel's furniture, and sat upon them. And Laban searched all the tent and found them not."

(33) Gen. 33:1. "And Jacob lifted up his eyes, and looked, and, behold, Esau came and with him four hundred men. And he devided the children unto Leah, and unto **Rachel,** and unto the two handmaids."

Gen. 33:2. "And he put the handmaides and their children foremost, and Leah and her children after, and **Rachel** and Joseph hindermost."

Gen. 33:7 "And Leah also with her children came near, and bowed themselves; and after came Joseph near and **Rachel**, and they bowed themselves;

1732bc.

(35) Gen. 35:16. "And they journeyed from Beth-el; and there vwas but a little way to come to Ephrath: and **Rachel** travailed, and she had hard labour.

1729bc.

Gen. 35:19. "And **Rachel** died, and was buried in the way to Ephrath, which is Beth-lehem."

Gen. 35:20. "And Jacob set a pillar upon her grave: that is the pillar of **Rachel's** grave until this day."

Gen. 35:24. "The son's of **Rachel;** Joseph, and Benjamin:

Gen. 35:25. "And the sons of Bilhah, **Rachel's** hanhmaid; Dan and Naphtali:"

1689bc.

(48) Gen. 48:7. "And as for me, when I came from Padan, **Rachel** died by me in the land of Canaan, in the way, when yet there was but a little way to come unto Ephrath: and I biried her there in the way of Ephrath, the same is Beth-lehem."

1312bc.

(236) **RUTH 4:11**"And all the people that were in the gate, and the elders, said, We are witnesses. The Lord make the woman that is come into thine house like **Rache**l and Leah, which two did build the house of Israel: and do thou worthily in Ephratah and be famous in Bethlehem."

1095bc.

(246) **1 SAM. 10:2** "When thou art departed from me to-day then thou shalt find two men by **Rachel's** sepullchre in the border of Benlamin at Zelzah; and they will say unto thee, The asses which thou wentest to seek are found: and lo, thy father hath left the care of the asses, and sorroweth for you, saying, What shall I do for my son?"

606bc.

(776) **JER. 31:15** "Thus saith the Lord; A voice was heard in Ramah lamentation, and bitter weeping; **Rachel** weeping for her children refused to be comforted for her children, because they were not."

26ad.

(931) **MATT. 2:18** "In Rama was there a voice heard, lamentation, and weeping, and great mourning, **Rachel** weeping for her children, and would not becomforted, because they are not."

RAHAB

1451bc.

(189) JOSH. 2:1. And Joshua the son of Nun sent out of Shittin two men to spy secretly, saying, Go view the land, even Jericho. And they went and came into anharlot's house, named **Rahab**, and lodged there."

JOSH. 2;3. "And the king of Jericho sent unto **Rahab** saying, Bring forth the men that are come to thee, which are entered into thine house: for they be come to search out all the country."

(193) JOSH 6:17. "And the city shall be accursed, even it, and all that are therein, to the Lord: only **Rahab** the harlot shall live, she and all that are with her in the house, because she hid the messengers that we sent."

JOSH. 6:23. "And the young men that were spies went in, and brought out out **Rahab**, and her father, and her mother, and her brethren, and all that she had; and they broughtout all her kindred, and left them without the camp of Iserel."

JOSH. 6:25."And Joshua saved **Rahab** the harlot alive; and her father's housrhold, and all that she had; and she dwelleth in Israel even unto this day; because she hid messengers which Joshua sent to spy out of Jericho."

REBECCA

ANNO
DOMINI
60

(1055) ROM. 9:10. And not only this; but when **Rebecca** also had conceived by one, even by our father, Isaac.

REBEKAH

1872bc.

(22) GEN. 22:23. "And Bethuel begat **Rebekah**: these eight Milcah did bear to Nahor, Abraham's brother."

1857bc.

(24) GEN. 24:15. "And it came to pass, before he had done speaking, that, behold **Rebekah** came out, who was born to Bethuel, son of Milcah, wife of Nahor. Abraham's brother, with her pitcher upon her shoulder."

GEN.24:29. "And **Rebekah** had a brother, and his name was Laban: and Laband ran out unto the man, unto the well,"

GEN.24:30. "And it came to pass, when he saw the earring and bracelets upon his sister's hands, and when he heard the words of **Rebekah** his sister, saying, Thus spake the man unto me; that he came unto the man; and behold, he stood by the camels at the well."

GEN.24:45. "And before I had done speaking in mine heart, behold, **Rebekah** came forth with her pitcher on her shoulder; and she went down unto the well, and drew water: and I said unto her, Let me drink, I pray thee."

GEN.24:51. "Behold, **Rebekah** is before thee, take her, and go, and let her be thy master's son's wife, as the alord hath spoken."

GEN.24:53. "And the servant brought forth jewels of silver, and jewels of gold, and raiment, and gave them to **Rebekah**: he gave also to her brother and to her mother precious things."

GEN.24:58. "And they called **Rebekah**, and they said unto her, Wilt thou go with this man? And she said, I will go."

GEN.24:59. "And they sent away **Rebekah** their sister, and her nurse, and Abraham"s servent, and his men."

GEN.24:60. "And they blessed **Rebekah**, and said unto her, Thou art our sister, be thou the mother of thousands of millions, and let thy seed possess the gate of those which hate them."

GEN.24:61. "And **Rebekah** arose, and her damsels, and they rode upon the camels, and followed the man: and the servent took **Rebekah**, and went his way."

GEN.24:64. "And **Rebekah** lifted up her eyes, and when she saw Isaac, she lighted off the camel."

GEN.24:67. "And Isaac brought her into his mother Sarah's tent, and took **Rebekah**, and she became his wife; and he loved her: and Isaac was comforted after his mother's death."

1857bc.

(25) GEN.25:20, "And Isaac was forty years old when he took **Rebekah** to wife, the daughter of Bethuel the Syrian of Padan-aram, the sister to Laban the Syrian:"

1838bc.

GEN.25:21. "And Isaac entreated the Lord for his wife; because she was barren: and the Lord was entreated of him, and **Rebekah** his wife conceived."

1837bc.

GEN.25:28. "And Isaac loved Esau, because he did eat of his venison: But **Rebekah** loved Jacob."

1804bc.

(26) GEN.26:7, "And the men of the place asked him of his wife; and he said, She is my sister: for he feared to say, She is my wife; lest the men of the place should kill me for **Rebekah**; because she was fair to look upon."

GEN.26:8, "And it came to pass, when he had been there a long time, that Abimelech king of the Philistines looked out at a window, and saw, and, behold, Isaac was sporting with **Rebekah** his wife."

GEN.26:35. "Which were a grief of mind unto Isaac and to **Rebekah**."

1760bc.

(27) GEN.27:6, "And **Rebekah** spake unto Jacob her son, saying, Behold, I heard thy father speak unto Esua, thy brother, saying, Behold, I heard thy father speak unto ESAU thy brother, saying, ..."

GEN.27:7. "bring me venison, and make me savoury meat, that I may eat, and blessthe before the Lord fefore my death."

GEN.27:11, "And Jacob said to **Rebekah** his mother, Behold Esau my brother is a hairy man, and I am a smooth man:"

GEN.27:15, "And **Rebekah** took goodly raiment of her eldest son Esau, which were with her in the house, and put them upon Jacob her youngest son;"

GEN.27:42, "And these words of Esau her elder son were told to **Rebekah**: and she sent and called Jacob her younger son, and said unto him, Behold, thy brother Esau, as touching thee, doth comfort himself, proposing to kill thee."

GEN.27:46. "**And Rebekah** said to Isaac, I am weary of my life because of my daughters of Heth, ; if Jacob take a wife of the daughters of Heth: if Jacob take wife of the daughters of Heth, such as these which are of the daughters of the land, what good shall my life do me?"

(28) GEN.28:5 "And Isaac sent away Jacob: and he went to Padan-aram unto Laban, son of Bethuel the Syrian, the brother of **Rebekah,** Jacob's and Esau's mother."

(29) GEN.29:12. "And Jacob told Rachel that he was her father's brother, and that he was **Rebekah's** son; and she ran and told her father."

1732bc.

(35) GEN.35:8. "But Deborah, **Rebekah's** nurse, died and she was buried beneath Bethel, under an oak: and the name of it was called Allon-bachuth".

1689bc.

(49) GEN. 49:31. "There they buried Abraham and Sarah his wife; there they buried Isaac and **Rebekah** his wife, and there I buried Leah."

REUMAH

1872bc.

(22) GEN. 22:24. "And his concubine, whose name was **Reumah,** she bare also Tebah, and Gaham, and Thahash, and Maachah."

RHODA

44ad.

(1030) ACTS. 12:13. "And as Peter knocked at the door of the gate, a damsel came to hearken, named **Rhoda.**"

RIZPAH

1053bc.

(270) 2 SAM. 3:7. "And Saul had a concubine, whose name was **Rizpah**, the daughter of Aiah: and Ish-bosheth said to Abner, Wherefore hast tho gone in unto my fathers concubine?"

1021bc.

(288) 2 SAM. 21:8. "But the king took the two sons of **Rizpah** the daughter of Aiah, whom she bare unto Saul, Armoni and Mephibosheth….."

1019bc.

2 SAM. 21:10. "And **Rizpah** the daughter of Aiah took sackcloth, and spread it for her upon the rock, from the beginning of harvest until water dropped upon them out of heaven, and suffered neither the birds of the air to rest on them by day, nor the beasts of the field by night."

2 SAM. 21:11 "And it was told David what **Rizpah** the daughter of Aiah the concubine of Saul had done"

RUTH

Daughter-in-law of NAOMI.

1312bc

(234) Ruth 2:2 "And **Ruth** the Moabitess said unto Naomi, Let me go to the field, and glean ears of corn after him in whose sight I shall find grace. And she said unto her, go, my daughter".

RUTH 4:13 "So Boas took **Ruth**, and she was his wife: and when he went in unto her, the Lord gave her conception, and she bare a son."

SALOME

She was the daughter of Herodias, Queen and wife of King Herod. However, King Herrod was not her father. Her father was the King's own brother, Philip, whom her mother had previously been married to. (For John, the Baotist had said unto Herod, "it is not lawful for thee to have thy brother's wife." Mark 6:18)

Salome later rmarried her father's half brother, Herod Philip, the Tetrarch of what is now Syria. Later she would marry the ruler of Lesser Armenia, Aristobulus.

Salome became the wife of Zebedee and mother of John the Evangelist and James the Great.

32ad

(963) Mark 6:22 "And when the daughter (Salome) of the said Herodias came in, and danced, and pleased Herod, and them that sat with him, the king said unto the damsel, Ask of me whatsoever thou wilt, and I give it thee."

Mark 6:23 "And he sware unto her, Whatsoever thou shalt ask of me, I will give it thee, unto the half of my kingdom."

Salome then went and told her mother what her stepfather had said. "What shall I ask?" And her mother said "The head of John the Baptist."

Salome then went stright away to the king saying "I will that thou give me, by and by, in a charger, the head of John the Baptist."

MARK 6:26 "And the king was exceeding sorry; yet for his oath's sake, and for the sakes which sat with him, he would not reject her."

MARK 6:27 "And immediately the king sent an executioner, and commanded his head to be brought: and he went and beheaded him in the prison;"

MARK 6:28 "And brought his head in a charger, and gave it to the damsel; and the damsel gave it to her mother."

Great.

She was at the crucifixion of Christ;

She was also one of the first to learn of the resurrection;

33ad.

(973) **Mark 16:1** " And when the Sabbath was past, Mary Magdalene, and Mary the mother of James, and **Salome,** had bought aweet spices, that they might come and anoint him."

SAPPHIRA

33ad.

(1023) **ACTS. 5:1.** "But a certain man named Ananias, with **Sapphira** his wife, sold a possession,"

Acts. 5:2. "And kept part of the price, (his wife also being privy to it,) and brought a certain part, and laid it at the apostles feet.

Acts. 5:3. But Peter said, Ananias, Why hath Satan filled thine hart to lie to the Holy Ghost, and to keep back part of the price of the land?

SARAH

Sarah was the wife of Abraham, also his half sister. Abraham's father was Terah, descendant of Shem. He was born about the time of Hammurabi, king of Babylonia, between 2000 and 1500 bc."

Still childless after many years, **Sarah** thought it was her fault she could not conceive. She was deaperate that her huaband's line would continue, she tried to get him to have a child with her Egyptian slave girl, Hagar".

1910bc.

(17) **GEN.17:15** "And God said unto Abraham, As for Sarai thy wife, thou shalt not call her name **Sarah**, but **Sarah** shall her name be."

1898bc.

(20) **GEN. 20:12** "And yet indeed she is my sister, she is the daughter of my father, but not the daughter of my mother; and she became my wife".

Still chilhless after many tears, Sarah thought it was her foult she could not conceive. She was desperate that her husband's line would not continue, she tried to get him to have a child with her Egyptian salve girl, Hagar

Gen. 20:14. "And Abimelech took sheep, and oxen, and men-servents, and women-servents, and gave them unto Abraham, and restored him **SaraH** his wife."

Gen. 20:16 1898 bc. "And unto to **Sarah** he said, Behold, I have given thy brother a thousand pieces of silver: behold, he is to thee a covering of the eyes, unto all are with thee, and with all other: thus she was reproved."

(21) **GEN.21:3** "And Abraham called, the name of his son that was born unto him, whom **Sarah** bare to him, Isaac".

Gen. 21:4 "Abraham circumcised his son Isaac, being eight days old, as God had commanded him."

1897bc.

Gen. 21:6 "And **Sarah** said , God hath made me laugh, so that all that hear will laugh with me:"

Gen. 21:7 "And she said, Who would have said unto Abraham that **Sarah** should have children suck? For I have born him a son in his old age."

Gen. 21:9 "And **Sarah** saw the son of Hagar the Egyptian, which she had born unto Abraham, mocking."

1706bc.

(46) GEN. 46:17 "And the sons of Asher; Jimnah, and Ishuah, and Isui, and Beriah, and **Serah** their sister. And the sons of Beriah; Heber, and Malchiel.**"**

1689bc.

(49) GEN. 49:31. "There they buried Abraham and **Sarah** his wife; there they buried Isaac and Rebekah his wife, and there I buried Leah."

1452bc.

(143) NUM. 26:46. "And the name of the daughter of Asher was **Sarah**."

1444bc.

(345) 1 CHRON.7:30. "The sons of Asher; Imnah, and Isuah,and Ishuai, and Beriah, and **Serah** their sister."

Note: In **Gen., Num**. and **Chron**. She is refered to as Ashers' daughter.

(In **Gen. 46:17** and **Chron. 7:30** her name is spelled with an "e". Where as in **Gen.49:31** and **Num. 26:46,** it's spelled with an "a".)

Also, between **Gen. 46:17** and **Chron. 7:30, 262 years** have lapsed.

SARAH 2

60ad.

In this date the Bible tells of a **Sarah** in......

(1055) Rom. 9:9. "For this is the word of promise, At this time I will come, and **Sarah** shall have a son.

SARAH 3

From the "Book of Jasher".

A. M. 2103.

Chap. 3-12 "Now so it came to pass, that **Sarah,** Abbraham's wife, had not brought forth her first-born."

Chap. 3-13, "And Abraham complained, and said; "Unto me thou hast not given an heir: Lo! The stranger in my house, shall rule after me**".**

Chap. 3-14 "And Abraham heard a voice saying unto him, "Circumcise the flesh of thy foreskin, for therefore art thou barren".

Chap. 3-15 "And Abraham did so: and he went in unto **Sarah**, and she conceived, and bare a son, and he called his name Isaac".

Chap. 3-16 "And Abraham was ninety and nine years old when he circumcised the flesh of his foreskin".

BOOK OF JASHER:

It was to have been part of the Bible but for some unknown reason was suppressed. Translating the book from the Hebrew into English by Alcuin, it was lost again. It was not until 1721, when a gentleman, traveling through the north of England discovered it. He had it in his possession until 1750 when he showed it to an Earl who saw it "as a work of great sincerity, plainness and truth". His lordship's opinion was that "it should have been placed in the Bible before the Book of Joshua" He further adds, " by a writing on the outside of the manuscript, it should seem that this translation was laid before our first reformers."

SARAI

1910bc.

(17) GEN.17:15 "And God said unto Abraham, As for **Sarai** thy wife, thou shalt not call her name Sarai, but Sarah shall her name be."

SHEBA

992bc.

(301) 1. Kings 10:1, "And when the queen of **Sheba** heard of the fame of Solomon concerning the name of the lord, she came to prove him with hard questions."

1 Kings 10:2 And she came to Jerusalem with a very great train, with camels that bare spices, and very much gold and precious stones: and when she was come to Solomon, she commaned with him of all that was in her heart."

1 Kings 10:6 "And she said to the king. "It was a true report that I heard in mine own land of thy acts and of thy wisdom."

1 Kings 10:13. "And king Solomon gave unto the Queen of **Sheba** all her desire, whatsoever she asked, besides that which Solomon gave her of his royal bounty.So she tutned and went to her own country, she and her servants."

(376) 2 CHRON. 9:1. "And when the queen of **Sheba** heard of the fame of Solomon, she came to prove Solomon with hard questions at Jerusalem, with a very great company, and camels that bare spices, and gold in abundance, and precious stones: and when she was come to Solomon, she communed with him of all that was in her heart."

2 CHRON.9:3. "And when the queen of **Sheba** had seen the wisdom of Solomon, and the house that he had built,...."

2 CHRON.9:9. "And she gave the king an hundred and twenty talents of gold, and of spices great abundance, and precious stones: neither was there any such spice as the queen of **Sheba** gave king Solomon."

2 CHRON. 9:12. :And king Solomon gave to the queen of **Sheba** all her desire, whatsoever she asked, besides that which she had brought unto the king. So she turned, and went away to her own land, she and her servants."

SHELOMITH

Of the tribe of Dan.

1490bc.

(114) **LEV. 24:11.** "And the Israelitish woman's son blasphemed the name of the Lord, and his mother's name was **Shelomith**, the daughter of Dibri, of the tribe of Dan:"

SHELOMITH 2

Daughter of Zerubbabel.

1053bc.

(341) **1 CHRON. 3:19,** "And the sons of Pedaiah were Zerubbabel, and Shimei: and the sons of Zerubbabel; Mmeshullam, and Hananiah, and **Shelomith** their sister:"

SHELOMITH 3

974bc.

(378) **2 CHRON. 11;20**. "And after her he took Maachah, the daughter of Abhsalom; which bare him Abijah, And Attai, and Zisa, and **Shelomith**."

SHERAH

1444bc.

(345) **1 CHRON. 7;24.** "And his daughter was **Sherah**, who built Beth-horon the nether, and the upper, and Uzzen-sherah."

SHIMEATH

839bc.

(325) 2 KINGS. 12:21. "For Jozachar the son of **Shimeath,** and Jehozabad the son of Shomer, his servants, smote him, and he died; and they buried him with his fathers in the city of David; and Amaziah his son reigned in his stead."

840bc.

2 CHRON .24:26. "And these are they that conspired against him; Zabad the son of **Shimeath** an Ammonitess, and Jehozabad the son of Shimrith a Mobitess."

SHIMRITH

840bc.

2 CHRON. 24:26. . "And these are they that conspired against him; Zabad the son of Shimeath an Ammonitess,and Jehozabad the son of **Shimrith** a Mobitess."

SHIPHRAH

1635bc.

(51) EXOD. 1:15. " And the king 0f Egypt spake to the Hebrew midwives (of Which the name of one was **Shiphrah,** and the name of the other Puah;)"

SHOMER

838bc.

(325) 2 KINGS. 12:21 "For Jozachar the son of Shimeath, and Jehozabad the son of **Shomer,** his servants smote him and he died; and they buried him with his fathers in the city of David: and Amaziah his son reigned in his stead."

SHUA

1444bc.

(345) 1 CHRON. 7;32. "And Heber begat Japhlet, and Shomer, and Hotham, and **Shua** their sister."

SHUNAMMITE

895bc.

(317) 2 KINGS. 4:12. "And he said to Gehazi, his servant, Call this **Shunammite**. And when he had called her, she stood before him."

SUSANNA

31ad.

(981) LUKE 8:3 "And Joanna the wife of Chuza, Herod's steward, and **Susanna,** and many others, which ministered unto him of their substance."

Being well educated and married to a wealthy man, named Joakim, she enjoyed living in a large house. She also had a beautiful garden where she liked to walk and, from time to time, would bathe. Because of her beauty, she had aroused some of the men of the town. One very hot day she desided to bathe in the garden. While anointing herself with oils, unaware that two of the local men were watching, they grabed her and said that if she didn't submit to them, they would tell her husband that she had been unfaithful to him. She didn't, they did and her husband believed them. Condemnd, she cried out to God for help. God heard her and sent Daniel to talk to Joakim, telling him at least he could do was to question the two men separately. He did so and found discrepancy in their stories. Susanna was cleared and the two men were found guilty and subsequently hanged.

SYNTYCHE

64ad.

(1107) PHIL. 4:2 I beseech Eruodias and beseech **Syntyche**, that they be of the same mind in the Lord.

TABITHA (DORCAS)

38ad.

(1027) ACTS. 9:36. "Now there was at Joppa a certain disciple named **Tabitha,** which by interpretation is called **Dorcas**; this woman was full of good works and alms-deeds which she did."

ACTS. 9:39. "Then Peter arose, and went with them. When he was come, they brought him into the upper chamber: and all the widows stood by him weeping, and shewing the coats and garments which **Dorcas** made, while she was with them."

ACTS. 9:40. "But Peter put them all forth, and kneeled down, and prayed; and turning him to the body, said **Tabitha**, arise. And she opened her eyes: and when she saw Peter, she sat up."

TAHPENES

984bc.

(302) 1 KINGS. 11:19. "And Hadad found great favour in the sight of Pharaoh, so that he gave him to wife the siater of his own wife, the sister of **Tahpenes** the queen."

1 KINGS. 11:20. "And the sister of Tahpenes bare him Genubath his son, whom **Tahpenes** weaned in Pharaoh's house: and Genubath was in Pharaoh's household among the son's of Pharaoh."

TAMAR

Judah's wife.

1727bc.

(38) **GEN. 38:6.** "And Judah took a wife for Er his first-born, whose name was **Tamar**."

GEN. 38:7. "And Er, Judah's first-first born, was wicked in the sight of the Lord; and the Lord slew him."

GEN. 38:11. "Then said Judah to **Tamar** his daughter-in-law, Remain a widow at thy father's house, till Shelah my son be grown; for he said, Lest peradventure he die also as his brethren did: and **Tamar** went and dwelt in her father's house."

GEN. 38:13. "And it was told **Tamar**, saying Behold, thy father-in-law goeth up to Timnath, to shear his sheep."

GEN. 38:24 "And it came to pass, about three months after, that it was told Judah, saying, **Tamar** thy daughter-in-law hath played the harlot; and also, behold, she is with child by whoredom. And Judah said, bring her forth, and let her be burnt."

TAMAR 2

1496bc.

(340) 1 CHRON. 2:4. "And **Tamar** his daughter-in-law bare him Pharez and Zerah. All the sons of Judah were five."

1330bc.

(280) 2 SAM. 13:22. "And Absalom spake unto his brother Amnon neither good nor bad: for Absalom hated Amnon, because he had forced his sister **Tamar**."

2 SAM. 13:32. "And Jonadab, the son of Shimeah, David's brother, answered and said, Let not my lord suppose that they have slain all the young men the king's sons; for Amnon only is dead: for by the appointment of Absalon this hath been determined from the day that he forced his sister **Tamar.**

1312bc.

(236) RUTH. 4:12. "And let the house be like the house Pharez, whom **Tamar** bare unto Juda, of the seed which the Lord shall give thee of this young woman."

TAMAR 3

David's daughter.

1053bc.

(341) **1 CHRON. 3:9.** "These were all the sons of David, beside the sons of the concubines, and **Tamar** their sister."

1032bc.

(280) **2 SAM. 13:1.** "And it came to pass after this, that Absalom the son of David had a fair sister, whose name was **Tamar**; and Amnon the son of David loved her."

2 SAM. 13:2. "And Amnon was so vexed, that he fell sick for his sister **Tamar**; for she was a vergin; and Amnon thought it hard for him to do any thing to her."

2 SAM. 13:3. "But Amnon had a friend, whose name was Jonadab, the son of Shimeah David's brother: and Jonadab was a very subtle man."

2 SAM. 13:4. "And he said unto him, Why art thou, being the king's son, lean from day to day? Wilt thou not tell me? And Amnon said unto him, I love **Tamar**, my brother's sister."

2 SAM. 13:5. "And Jonadab said unto him, Lay thee down on thy bed, and make thyself sick: and when thy father cometh to see thee, say unto him, I pray thee, let my sister **Tamar** come, and give me meat, and dress the meat in my sight, that I may see it, and eat it at her hand."

2 SAM. 13:6. "So Amnon lay down, and made himself sick: and when the king was come to see him, Amnon said unto the king, I pray thee, Let **Tamar** my sister come, and make me a couple of cakes in my sight, that I may eat at her hand."

2 SAM. 13:7. "Then David sent home to **Tamar**, saying, go now to thy brother Amnon's house, and dress him some meat."

2 SAM.13:8. "So **Tamar** went to her brother Amnon's house; and he was laid down. And she took flour, and kneaded it, and made cakes in his sight, and did bake the cakes."

2 SAM. 13:10. "And Amnon said unto **Tamar**, Bring the meat into my chamber, that I may eat of thine hand. And **Tamar** took the cakes which she had made, and brought them into the chamber to Amnon her brother."

2 SAM. 13:11. "And when she had brought them unto him to eat, he took hold of her, and said unto her, Come lie with me my sister."

2 SAM. 13:12. "And she answered him, Nay, my brother, do not force me; for no such thing ought to be done in Israel: do not thou this folly."

2 SAM. 13:14. "Howbeit, he would not hearken unto her voice: but being stronger than she, forced her, and lay with her."

2 SAM. 13:15. "Then Amnon hated her exceedingly; so that the hatred wherewith he hated her was greater than than the love wherewith he had loved her. And Amnon said unto her, Arise, be gone."

2 SAM. 13:19. And **Tamar** put ashes on her head, and rent the garments of divers colours that was on her, and laid her hand on her head, and went on crying."

2 SAM. 13:20. "And Absalon her brouther said unto her, Hath Amnon thy brother been with thee? but hold now thy peace, my sister: he is thy brother; regard not this thing. So **Tamar** remained desolate in her brother Absalom's house."

1027bc.

(281) **2 SAM. 14:27.** "And unto Absalon there were born three sons, and one daughter, hose name was **Tamar**; she was a woman of a fair countenance."

TAPHATH

King Solomams' daughter

1014bc.

(295) 1 KINGS. 4:11. "The son of Abinadab, in all the region of Dor; which had **Taphath** the daughter of Solomon to wife:"

THAMAR

About the sixth year before
the Common Acount called
Anno Domini. (1530)

(930) MATT.1:3. "And Jadas begat Phares and Zara of **Thamar**; and Phares begat Esrom; and Esrom begat Aram."

TIMNA

1740BC.

(36) GEN. 36:12. "And **Timna** was the concubine to Eliphaz, Esau's son; and she bare to Eliphaz, Amalek: these were the sons of Adah, Esau's wife."

GEN. 36:22. "And the children of Lotan were Hori, and Herman: and Lotan's sister was **Timna**."

1676bc.

(339) 1 CHRON. 1:39. "And the sons of Lotan; Hori, and Homan: and **Timna** was Lotan's sister."

TIRZAH

1452bc.

(143) **NUM. 26:33.** "And Zelophehad the son of Hepher had no sons, but daughters: and the names of the daughters of Zelophehad were Mahlah, and Noah, Hoglah, Milcah, and **Tirzah**."

(1444) **NUM. 27:1.** "Then came the daughters of Zelophehad, the son of Hepher, the son of Gilead, the son of Machir, the son of Manasseh, of the families of Manasseh the son of Joseph: and these are the names of his daughters; Mahlah, Noah, and Hoglah, and Milcah, and **Tirzah**."

(153) **NUM. 36:11.** "For Mahalah, **Tirzah,** and Hoglah, and Milcah, and Noah, the daughters of Zelophehad, were married unto their father's brothers' sons:"

1444bc.

(204) **JOSH. 17:3** "But Zelophehad, the son of Hepher, the son of Gilead, the son of Machir, the son Manasseh, had no sons, but daughters,: and these are names of his daughters, Mahlah, and Noah, Hoglah, Milcah, and **Tirzah**."

TRYPHENA

60ad.

(1062) **ROM. 16:12.** "Salute **Tryphena** and Tryphosa, who labour in the Lord. Salute the beloved Peris which laboured much in the Lord."

TRYPHOSA

(1062) **ROM. 16:12.** "Salute Tryphena and **Tryphosa**, who labour in the Lord. . Salute the beloved Persis which laboured much in the Lord."

VASHTI

619bc.

(427) ESTHER 1:9. "Also **Vashti** the queen made a feast for the women in the royal house which belonged to king Ahasuerus."

ESTHER 1:11. "To bring **Vashti** the queen before the king with the crown royal, to show the people and the princes her beauty: for she was fair to look on."

ESTHER 1:12. But the queen **Vashti** refused to come at the king's commandment by his chamberlains: therefore was the king very wroth, and his anger burned in him.."

ESTHER 1:15. "What shall we do unto the queen **Vashti** according to law, because she hath not performed the commandment of the king Ahasuerus by the chamberlains?"

ESTHER 1:16. "And Memucan answered before the king and the princes, **Vashti** the queen hath not done wrong to the king only, but also to all the princes, and to all the people that are in all the provinces of the king Ahasuerus."

ESTHER 1:17. "For this deed of the queen shall come aboard unto all women, so that they shall despise their husbands in their eyes, when it shall be reported, The king Ahasuerus commanded **Vashti** the queen to be brought in before him, but she came not."

ESTHER 1:19. "If it please the king, let there go a royal commandment from him, and let it be written among the laws of the Persians and the Medes, that it be not altered, That **Vashti** come no more before Ahasuerus: and let the king give her royal estate unto another that is better than she."

(428) ESTHER 2:1. "After these things, when the wrath of king Ahasuerus was appeased, he remembered **Vashti**, and what she had done, and what was decreed against her."

ZEBUDAH

610bc.

(336) 2 KINGS 23:36. Jehoiakim was twenty and five years old when he began to reign; and he reigned eleven years in Jerusalem. And his mother's name was **Zebudah,** the daughter of Pedaiah of Rumah."

ZERESH

610bc.

(431) ESTHER 5:10. "Never the less, Haman refrained himself: and when he came home, he sent and called for his friends, and **Zeresh** his wife."

ESTHER 5:14. "Then said **Zeresh** his wife and all his friends unto him, Let a gallows be made of fifty cubits high, and to-morrow speak thou unto the king that Mordecai may be hanged thereon:…….."

ZERUAH

984bc.

(302) 1 KINGS 11:26. "And Jeroboam the son of Nebat, an Ephrathite of Zereda, Solomon's servant, whose mother's name was **Zeruah**, Solomon's servant,……"

ZERUIAH

David's half sister and Abigail's sister.

1060bc.

(262) 1 SAM. 26:6. "Then answerd David and said to Ahimelsch the Hittite, and to Abishai the son of **Zeruiah**, brother of Jacob, saying, who will go down with me to Saul to the camp?......"

1060bc.

(269) 2 SAM.2:13. "And Joab the son of **Zeruiah**, and the servents of David went out, and met together by the pool of Gebeon: and they sat down, the one on the one side of the pool and the other on the othrt side of the pool."

2 SAM. 2:18. "And there were three sons of **Zeruiah** there, Jab, and Abishai, and Asahel: and Ashael was as light of foot as a wild roe."

1055bc.

2 SAM. 2:13 "And Joab the son of **Zeruiah**, and servants of David went out and together and met together by the pool of Gibeon:......"

2 SAM 2:18. And there were three sons of **Zeruiah** there, Joab, and Abisahai: and Asahel; and Asahel was as light of foot as a wild roe."

1048bc.

(270) 2 SAM 3:39. "And I am this day weak, through anointed king; and these men the sons of **Zeruiah** be too hard foe me. The Lord shall reward the doer of evil according to his wickedness."

1040bc.

(275) **2 SAM. 8:16.** And Joab the son of **Zeruiah** was over the host; and Johoshaphat the son of Ahilud was recorder;'

1027bc.

(281) **2 SAM 14:1.** "Now Joab the son of **Zeruiah** perceived that the king's heart was toward Absalom."

1023bc.

(283) **2 SAM. 16:9.** "Then said Abishai the son of **Zeruiah** unto the king, Why should this dead dog curse my lord the king? Let me go over, I pray thee, and take off his head."

2 SAM .16:10. "And the king said, What have I to do with you, ye sons of **Zeruiah**? So let him curse, because the Lord hath said unto him, curse David......"

(284) **2 SAM. 17:25** "And Absalom made Amasa captain of the host instead of Joab; which Amasa was a man's son whose name Ithra, an Israelite, that went in to Abigail the daughter of Nahash, sister to **Zeruiah**, Joab's mother."

(285) **2 SAM. 18:2.** "And David sent forth a third part of the people under the hand of Joab, and a third part under the hand of Abishai the son of **Zeruiah**......."

(286) **2 SAM. 19:21.** "But Abishai the son of **Zeruiah** answered and said, Shall not Shmei be put to death for this, because he cursed the Lord's anointed?"

2 SAM. 19:22 "And David said, What have I to do with you ye sons of **Zeruiah,** that ye should this day be adversaries unto me?......."

1019bc.

)288) **2 SAM. 21:17'**. "But Abishai the son of **Zeruiah** succoured him, and smote the Philistine, and killed him……"

1018bc.

(290) 2 SAM. 23:18. "And Abishai, the brother of Joab, the son of **Zeruiah,** was chief amoung three. And he lifted up his spear against three hundred, and slew them, and had the name among three."

ZIBIAH

878bc.

(325) 2 KINGS 12:1. "In the seventh year of Jehu, Jehoash began to reign; and forty years reigned he in Jerusalem. And his mother's name was **Zibiah** of Beer-sheba."

(391) 2 CHROM. 24:1 "Joash was seven years old when he began to reign, and he reigned fourty years in Jerusalem. His mother's name also was **Zibiah** of Beer-sheba."

ZILLAH;

3875bc.

(4) Gen.4:19 "And Lamech took unto him two wives: the name of the one was Adah, and the name of the other **Zillah**"….

Gen, 4:22 "And **Zillah**, she also bare Tubal-cain, an instructor of every artificer in brass and iron; and the sister of Tubal-cain was Naamah."

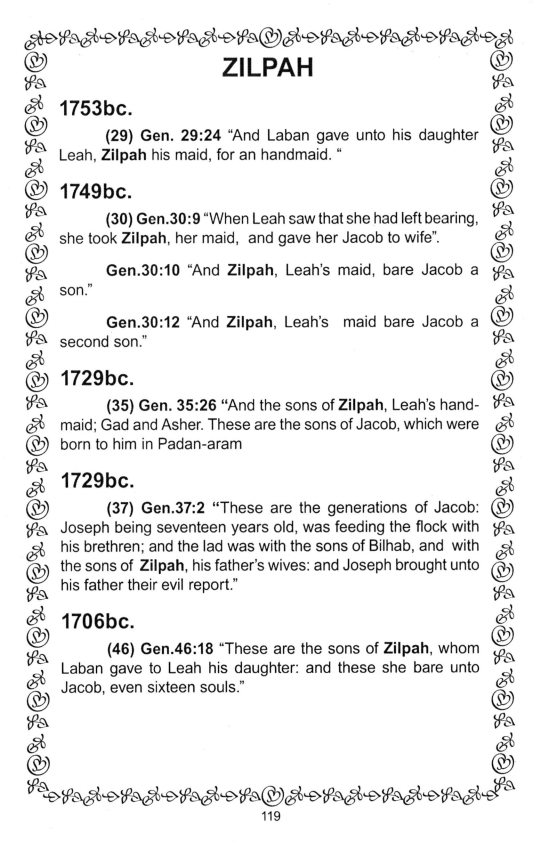

ZILPAH

1753bc.

(29) **Gen. 29:24** "And Laban gave unto his daughter Leah, **Zilpah** his maid, for an handmaid. "

1749bc.

(30) **Gen.30:9** "When Leah saw that she had left bearing, she took **Zilpah**, her maid, and gave her Jacob to wife".

Gen.30:10 "And **Zilpah**, Leah's maid, bare Jacob a son."

Gen.30:12 "And **Zilpah**, Leah's maid bare Jacob a second son."

1729bc.

(35) **Gen. 35:26** "And the sons of **Zilpah**, Leah's hand-maid; Gad and Asher. These are the sons of Jacob, which were born to him in Padan-aram

1729bc.

(37) **Gen.37:2** "These are the generations of Jacob: Joseph being seventeen years old, was feeding the flock with his brethren; and the lad was with the sons of Bilhab, and with the sons of **Zilpah**, his father's wives: and Joseph brought unto his father their evil report."

1706bc.

(46) **Gen.46:18** "These are the sons of **Zilpah**, whom Laban gave to Leah his daughter: and these she bare unto Jacob, even sixteen souls."

ZIPPORAH

Wife of Moses

1531bc.

(52) **EXOD. 2:20.** And he (Jethro) said unto his daughters, And where is he? Why is it that you have left the man? Call him, that he may eat bread.

EXOD. 2:21 "And Moses was content to dwell with this man: and he gave Moses, **Zipporah** his daughter."

1491bc.

(54) **EXOD. 4:25.** "And **Zipporah** took a sharp stone and cut off the foreskin of her son, and cast it at his (Moses') feet., and said: Surely a bloody husband art thou to me."

(68) **EXOD. 18:2.** "Then Jethro, Moses' father-in-law, took **Zipporah**, Moses' wife, after he had sent her back."

WOMEN INDEX

About the Author

Charles Douglas Greer
From the onset he was called "Doug"
Born in Ottawa, Canada, in 1921.
Both parents from Scotland.
Moved to California in 1924.
Settled in Glendale.
In 1928 won a freckled-face contest.
Because of this he got work in the movies.
His first days work was in a crowd screen in one of the first
talking pictures,
"Sunny side Up". 1929
He was a member of the Screen Actors Guild, #11732
He worked with Jackie Copper in many of the "Our Gang"
comedies as well as
with Mickey Rooney in the "Mickey McGuire Comedies".
As a teenager, he worked again with Jackie Copper
in "When a Feller Needs a Friend", M G M.
After working on many pictures
and meeting many movie stars,
it was time to move on.
This inappropriate career he had as a young man
was not for him.
It had interfered with his education
While attending Burbank High School,
"Doug" studied Aircraft Sheet Metal.
When he graduated he went to work for Lockheed Aircraft
Company in Burbank, Ca.
World War II having started, he volunteered for and joined the
Tenth Mountain Divison,
the Ski Troops. (He had learned to ski in the
mountains of California.)
When his Battalion prepared for overseas service,
he was transferred to "Inactive Duty" to go back to Lockheed
for a specific job.
When this was finished, June 8th, 1944,

he was called back into service with the 1267th Combat Engineer Battalion.
He "visited" England, France, Luxemburg and Germany.
When the war in Germany was over,
he went to Marseille, France.
There he boarded a ship that took him
through the Panama Canal
and ended up in the Philippine Islands, as part
of an invasion force to go to Japan.
While in the Philippines, he contacted Malaria.
He was Honorably Discharged June 8,1946.
After the war he went to work for Laboratory Furniture Company, Burbank, California.
There he learned the ins and outs of the trade.
He formed his own Corporation, "American Northern",
specializing in Fume Hoods and their exhaust systems.
He was married for 40 years, 7 months, 7.days.
He lost her Jan. 30,1990.
Retired, he lives in Scotts Valley, Ca.

Printed in the United States
71004LV00005B/174

9 781425 963736